Questions of
counselling and therapy

Questions of ethics in counselling and therapy

Caroline Jones (contributing editor)
Carol Shillito-Clarke
Gabrielle Syme
Derek Hill
Roger Casemore
Lesley Murdin

Open University Press
Buckingham · Philadelphia

Open University Press
Celtic Court
22 Ballmoor
Buckingham
MK18 1XW

email: enquiries@openup.co.uk
world wide web: www.openup.co.uk

and
325 Chestnut Street
Philadelphia, PA 19106, USA

First Published 2000

ISBN   0 335 20610 7 (pb)   0 335 20611 5 (hb)

A catalogue record of this book is available from the British Library

Library of Congress Cataloging-in-Publication Data Available

Copy-edited and typeset by The Running Head Limited,
www.therunninghead.com
Printed in Great Britain by The Cromwell Press, Trowbridge

To Tony, with love

Contents

behaviour that have reduced her to a very debilitated state. Yet she adores him and has no complaint. It is he who complains that she is untrustworthy. He shows no awareness of the harm being done to his partner, nor of his coercive behaviour. What ethical issues require consideration?

Neil is confined to a wheelchair and has an untreatable degenerative condition. He and partner Doug seek couple counselling and make it apparent that they want to set up a contract between them which would lead Doug to give Neil a lethal dose of drugs when Neil appears no longer to be able to tolerate his own deterioration. The counsellor is asked to monitor negotiation between the partners to ensure that no hidden agendas distort the contract both say they want. What ethical issues require consideration?

What are a counsellor's responsibilities when an adult client discloses childhood sexual abuse and where the perpetrator(s) may still be abusing?

At assessment, a potential client tells me she has been seeing another counsellor for some time but wants to make a change – the other counsellor is unaware of this so how should I proceed?

Are there ethical as well as practical issues about keeping case-notes?

What are the ethical considerations when a former client persists with unwanted contact?

How might the ethical issues when counselling children and young people be different from when working with adults?

What are my responsibilities when I suspect another counsellor is behaving unethically?

standards but he disputes this. Am I responsible for his
mistakes or his future development or work with clients?

Acknowledgements

As editor, I wish to thank the other authors for all their help and encouragement during the creation and production phases. Collectively, we thank those who have supported us during the process. Writing, like counselling and therapy, is a solitary activity that has taken us away from family and friends for long periods. The practical and emotional support of those at home with each of us is very much appreciated and we record our heartfelt thanks. Thanks also to all those who commented on drafting, assisted with research and listened when we wanted to talk through points to clarify thinking. In particular, thanks to Michael Jacobs, who started the ball rolling. His support, encouragement and experience were invaluable, especially to me.

In writing this book we have drawn upon a huge body of experience and learning from hundreds of practitioners and thousands of clients. We have also drawn upon our own experiences of working through similar questions and dilemmas. Such learning processes are rarely comfortable and have a profound effect on developing practice. For all of us, the learning continues.

Caroline Jones

Abbreviations

AHPP	Association of Humanistic Psychology Practitioners
BAC	British Association for Counselling
BAP	British Association of Psychotherapists
BASRT	British Association for Sexual and Relationship Therapy
BCP	British Confederation of Psychotherapists
BPS	British Psychological Society
CICA	Criminal Injuries Compensation Authority
COSCA	Confederation of Scottish Counselling Agencies
CPD	continuing professional development
DCoP	Division of Counselling Psychology
EAP	Employee Assistance Programme
POPAN	Prevention of Professional Abuse Network
UKCP	United Kingdom Council for Psychotherapy
UKRC	United Kingdom Register of Counsellors

List of contributors

Roger Casemore Roger is a Senior Teaching Fellow and Director of Counselling Courses at the University of Warwick and runs a small private counselling practice which he has maintained for over 30 years. He is a past Chair of BAC and has chaired BAC's Complaints Committee and has been the President of Counselling in Education for 15 years.

Derek Hill Originally a physicist, Derek worked in education for 14 years world-wide. Counselling with Relate led to work as a supervisor, a trainer, its Head of Counselling and, latterly, its Head of Practitioner Training. Derek was a member of BAC's Complaints Committee and one of its trustees for five years. He is a Fellow of BAC.

Caroline Jones Caroline is an employee counsellor with 16 years' experience in this setting. From 1991 to 1998 she served on BAC's Standards and Ethics Committee, chairing for the final 15 months. She is a BAC accredited counsellor and Fellow of BAC. She also has a small independent practice as a counselling supervisor.

Lesley Murdin Lesley is a psychoanalytic psychotherapist and psycho-dynamic counsellor with a private practice in Cambridge. She is a BAC accredited trainer and is the Chair of the Psychotherapy Training Committee at the Westminster Pastoral Foundation. She is past Chair of the UKCP Ethics Committee and writes and lectures on psycho-therapy and counselling.

Carol Shillito-Clarke Carol is a Chartered Counselling Psychologist and BAC accredited counsellor and supervisor. Over the past 25 years she has trained and worked as an integrative therapist, supervisor, trainer, lecturer and consultant in both the private and public sectors. She has a private practice in Warwick.

Gabrielle Syme   Gabrielle has worked as a counsellor for almost 30 years, initially as a volunteer, then in higher education and currently in independent practice. She has chaired ASC, BAC's Standards and Ethics Committee and BAC. Her special interests are bereavement and good practice reflected in *Gift of Tears* and *Counselling in Independent Practice*. She is a Fellow of BAC and a BAC accredited counsellor and supervisor.

Introduction

This book aims to explore and describe our thinking about what constitutes ethics in practice in individual and couple counselling and counselling-related activities, through the exploration of a number of questions. The book is written for a wide readership – trainees, practising counsellors and therapists, trainers and counselling supervisors, employers and service providers, those people who have sought or are thinking of seeking counselling or therapy and those with a more general interest in the profession.

The largest section of the book looks at questions of ethics in practice for counsellors and therapists, starting from the stand-point of the British Association for Counselling, which considers there is no generally accepted distinction between counselling and psychotherapy (BAC 1997: 3.3). For those seeking more specific definitions of these activities see Appendix 1. Counselling, psychotherapy and counselling psychology, as activities, do not exist in isolation, however, and there are also sections looking at questions of ethics in training, counselling supervision and research and at more general issues of interest. Counselling, psychotherapy and counselling psychology are practised in settings (agency, institution or independent practice) which in turn influence the work and, to some extent, the kinds of ethical dilemmas that can arise in practice. Examples of this will arise throughout the book.

All the contributors to this book belong to one or more professional associations and these memberships clearly inform our practice. Our aim is to explore issues and offer thoughts from a range of perspectives. Some questions focus on occasions where there are conflicting ethical priorities and where there may be no guidance from codes.

Finally, we are aware of those who have reservations about the activities of counselling and psychotherapy. The authors share the perspective that when counselling and therapy are provided in an ethical way, that is, non-exploitative, non-abusive and appropriate to the needs of the client at the time when undertaken, these are of benefit to many clients. The aim of this book is to offer individual opinions on ethical and thoughtful practice.

Guide for readers

- The contributors make reference to codes, guidelines and the law, all of which are subject to change. Therefore readers are reminded that it is wise to check whether any code or guideline has been revised since the publication of this book (Appendix 2), and to keep up with changes in the law and European Union Directives as these occur. The contributors have made every effort to be accurate about information.
- The book focuses on ethics in practice in face-to-face counselling and related activities. Counselling by telephone and counselling using modern communicative technologies raise additional practice issues, although the ethical principles discussed throughout the book apply.
- The term 'practitioner' is used when referring to those who hold more than one role in the profession and to avoid repetition of the words counsellor and therapist. The word 'profession' includes all practitioners whether paid or working voluntarily and whether working for a few hours a week or 'full time'.
- Nothing turns on the genders used in the questions and answers.
- The United Kingdom has a multiracial, multicultural society and the terms 'white' and 'black' are used for the majority and minority ethnic populations. This recognizes that skin colour influences the ways that individuals are treated and therefore experience life.
- All vignettes used to illustrate points are fictitious.
- Abbreviations quoted throughout the book are listed on p. xiv, to avoid repetition.

SECTION 1

An overview of ethics relating to counselling and therapy

Ethics – '1 the science of morals in human conduct.
2a moral principles; rules of conduct. b a set of these'
(The Concise Oxford Dictionary)

Counselling – defined by the British Association for
Counselling (BAC) as a task where a client is given the
opportunity 'to explore, discover and clarify ways of
living more resourcefully and toward greater well-being'.
(BAC 1979)

The purpose of this section is to demonstrate the connections between universal moral principles, counselling values and ethical principles of counselling and all aspects of professional practice. Ethics in counselling is not an abstract or academic issue. It is a necessary and active thread that runs throughout every aspect of practice with the intention of acting at all times in the best therapeutic interests of clients as members of society.

Unethical and bad practice cause harm and distress, whereas good practice, by definition, normally does no harm. Good practice in counselling depends on all elements of the profession working together in harmony. These elements are the core task of counselling and the related tasks of training, continuing professional development, monitoring, evaluation and research and counselling supervision. At a wider level, there are the elements of the promotion of counselling as a useful and desirable contribution to the emotional health and well-being of members of society and the regulation of the profession and its practitioners, through registration and disciplinary procedures.

Elements of the profession

The counselling relationship and its setting

Counselling cannot guarantee that it will help every client. Effectiveness depends on many factors, including the counsellor's competence, trust in the relationship, the appropriateness of this kind of help at the time it is undertaken, the theoretical approach(es) used by the counsellor and the expectations and commitment of the client.

At an assessment interview, or during a first session, it is proper to establish with clients that it is their own choice to attend, that counselling is an appropriate way of helping with the difficulties presented and that the counsellor's particular way of working will be helpful to the client. This assessment is based on an understanding of why and when someone seeks counselling. Hooper suggests that 'on balance, people do not seek help if they believe they are normal unless *either* their capacity starts to break down *or* they experience bodily symptoms which concern them' (Hooper 1996: 637).

Many clients come into counselling feeling vulnerable, hence the importance in ethical practice of establishing a contract. During the counselling relationship, clients need to feel safe and counsellors provide for this by behaving in ways that are non-exploitative and by setting clear boundaries that positively demonstrate the sense of trustworthiness. Counsellors must also be therapeutically sensitive to clients. Even when working in a professional, non-exploitative and ethical way, there is the risk of unintended unkindness or abuse that leaves the clients more hurt and damaged than when they arrived. One example of this is when the counsellor remains silent with the aim of encouraging the client to speak of their difficulties but this is experienced by the client as threatening (Walker 1993). Another example concerns the caution necessary about focusing on strong feelings when this may be dangerous for clients with certain medical conditions (Palmer 1999). Endings, whether after a single session, a short contract or longer-term work, need to be managed effectively. While it may be clear that a therapeutic relationship has completed its active working phase because no further sessions are anticipated or have been booked, a counsellor may sometimes need to explain why any subsequent contact might diminish the achievements of counselling, should a client propose this contact.

When people meet for the first time, their observable characteristics make an impression, positive or otherwise, based on factors ranging from accent to appearance. In counselling, as elsewhere, this works both ways, as counsellor and client take first impressions of each other. Assumptions about each other might arise from this. Ethical practice includes commitment by the counsellor to be aware of bias and to work in non-discriminatory ways. Assumptions are best kept as imperfect generalizations, not developing into stereotypes, defined as rigid preconceptions held about all people who are members of a particular group, whether that group is defined along racial, religious, sexual or other lines (Sue and Sue 1990). Differences between counsellor and client may require open exploration during the counselling, so that the client is clear about the counsellor's attitudes.

Availability of counselling depends upon a person's circumstances, geography and accessibility. Counselling is available in various and distinct settings: voluntary agencies such as Relate; institutions providing services such as colleges and universities, workplaces, general practices or other National Health Service clinics; and independent (private) practice. Access to counselling, therefore, is free at the point of delivery if you are a student or an employee or a patient where a counselling service is available. Alternatively, it may be dependent on donations to a voluntary agency, or require payment of fees per session when seeing an independent practitioner. Currently, private counselling and psychotherapy services are disproportionately located in London and the south-east of England (Syme 1994; McMahon 1997). Accessibility of face-to-face counselling depends on services being within travelling distance and at premises that accommodate those with disabilities.

Clients need to be informed about the advantages and constraints of the setting they have chosen for counselling. Some key points are listed in Figure 1. These will be explored in greater detail in some of the questions throughout the book.

Monitoring, evaluation and research

The professions of counselling and psychotherapy are engaged in ongoing research to demonstrate how and when their work positively helps clients. This is the responsibility of the profession, and one to which every practitioner can contribute. Individually, there are benefits from the monitoring and evaluation of client work. This contributes towards competence and good practice as do further training, continuing professional development and supervision. Individual counsellors need to know which aspects of their own work are least and most effective, in addition to the relative merits of the different theoretical approaches with particular client groups or issues.

Aspect of counselling	Voluntary agency	Institutional service	Independent practice (sole practitioner or group)
Counsellor status	usually unpaid volunteer	salaried or sessional	self-employed
Client access	subject to availability and may require contributions	subject to eligibility	subject to affordability
Presenting problem	specialist issue or any issue	normally any issue	normally any issue
Funding of service	donations grants contributions	institution funds	clients pay fees
Limits to number of sessions	may set limits	may set limits	counsellor choice
Confidentiality limits extra to codes	usually within agency and may be constrained by funding	may have extra limits e.g. reports in connection with client work	counsellor choice
Supervision/ training/CPD	usually provided by agency	usually provided or funded	funded by counsellor
Theoretical approach(es)	may be according to agency preference	may be according to institution preference	counsellor choice
Complaints	agency may have procedure	institution may have procedure	when in membership of a professional association

Figure 1 Differences arising from settings, for counsellors and clients

Training

Those who undertake to provide training hold a responsibility to the profession and to society for the selection of trainees and their training to an adequate level for practice as counsellors. Selection and assessment tasks require the ability to make impartial judgements on the suitability and competence of others. Training may be undertaken by voluntary agencies or academic institutions or by independent (private) agencies. Levels and standards vary and it does not necessarily follow that an academically qualified counsellor is any more effective than one trained through other routes. Trainers have a responsibility to assess the suitability of trainees as counsellors at the beginning, during and at the end of the course and this can cause dilemmas, when the funding and viability of courses depend on numbers.

Counselling supervision

Those who undertake the task of counselling supervision (different from line-management supervision, which might also be undertaken in an agency or institutional setting) are normally experienced counsellors themselves or experienced practitioners in an allied field. They too hold a share of the responsibility to the profession and to society for 'quality control'. They act as a safeguard against unsuitable practice, such as when a counsellor is working beyond the limits of their competence or when their functioning is affected. They also have responsibility for taking action if they have concerns about the suitability of the supervisee as a counsellor. The actual process of supervision involves an ethical dilemma, as discussing client work with another is technically a breach of confidentiality. It is generally held that if conducted properly, the public interest in maintaining standards of safe practice outweighs the breach of confidentiality (Bond 1993).

The regulation and promotion of counselling

Membership and registration

The numbers of practitioners holding membership of a professional association have grown rapidly over the past decade. Professional associations each have an identity and usually develop their own codes, to the benefit of the members and the wider public. Codes can at the same time be 'rules of conduct' and educative (Palmer Barnes 1998). Sometimes, as well as having organizational membership of one of the professional associations listed in Appendix 2, some agencies and institutions have their own additional sets of rules and codes. These take account of the specialist nature of the counselling provided. This can be confusing for clients and when contracting counsellors need to be open about any constraints arising from these circumstances. The importance of membership, for clients, is in the access to complaints procedures and the opportunity to voice dissatisfactions.

The development of a United Kingdom Register for Counsellors

(UKRC) is a step towards statutory registration and a contribution towards the promotion of professionally delivered counselling. The requirements of registration include holding qualifications, maintaining standards of practice, continuing professional development, maintaining experience, undergoing continued supervision and holding professional liability insurance. The UKRC is a useful resource for those seeking counselling.

Managing complaints

Currently, public confidence in counselling and the profession depends on the degree to which practitioners are trusted to regulate themselves because at this time there is no statutory regulation of counsellors. Most disciplinary matters are dealt with internally by the professional associations or through the courts. The professional associations normally rely on expertise from within their membership to undertake the tasks of assessing the competence of other members or judging their practice in the event of a complaint. Experience over the past 20 years has increased understanding of the difference between mistakes, poor practice, negligence and malpractice (Palmer Barnes 1998).

Promotion of counselling

Activities that promote counselling include working in partnership with the media to enhance understanding of its benefits to the general public. An example is the series produced jointly by the BBC and Relate, which illustrated counselling and supervision in action (1996–7). It is also important to challenge misconceptions or unfounded criticisms of the profession and to acknowledge and take account publicly of any justified concerns. The profession should promote the benefits of counselling in ways that attract the resources needed to widen access to counselling to all groups in society who require it. Unrestricted numbers of training courses result in many newly trained counsellors competing for clients and jobs. This leads to an important question about the minimum volume of work that counsellors should undertake on a regular basis in order to retain their skills and increase their experience. BAC's individual counsellor accreditation (registration) scheme requires a minimum of 150 hours of counselling per annum from applicants and accredited counsellors. This is particularly important for clients in terms of quality and a higher number of practice hours per annum is recommended, together with a turnover of clients that is congruent with the theoretical approach used by the counsellor. There is a dilemma about how to ensure quality (minimum standards) without making entry to the profession unnecessarily restrictive. Clearly, increasing the availability of affordable, accessible counselling to those who require this benefits both counsellors and clients.

Ethics in counselling

The universal moral principles of

- beneficence – achieving the greatest good,
- non-maleficence – causing least harm,
- justice – what is fairest,
- respecting autonomy – maximizing opportunities for all to implement their choices, and
- law – what is legal

are principles used as standards in the drafting of codes of practice and guidelines and are benchmarks used to weigh up options when faced with matters not covered by codes and ethical dilemmas.

Ethical values and principles of counselling

Ethical principles of counselling arise out of the universal moral principles and the more specific values of counselling: *integrity, impartiality* and *respect*. Many codes make specific reference to these, which underpin four key ethical principles in counselling:

- responsibility – accountability and competence,
- purposefulness – contracting,
- trustworthiness – non-discriminatory approach and boundaries, and
- confidentiality – the highest levels of confidentiality possible according to the law and the setting.

Responsibility means being responsible *to* clients, the profession and society. Counsellors do not take responsibility *for* clients, as the autonomy or self-determination of clients is important, as long as this does not infringe the rights of others. Counsellors are, however, responsible for the work undertaken with clients.

Purposefulness emphasizes that counselling is an activity that is undertaken deliberately and voluntarily by both parties. This can distinguish counselling from some other forms of helping (BAC 1991). Clients determine the aims and goals of counselling.

Trustworthiness indicates a relationship that is separate from social and other networks, within which clients feel safe to explore feelings and issues without fear of criticism and in an atmosphere of impartiality and respect.

Confidentiality refers to the duty to provide privacy undertaken by the counsellor towards clients and former clients. The content and personal details disclosed during counselling remain private at the time and afterwards, extending beyond the death of clients and the retirement of counsellors, limited only by constraints of law and setting.

These principles are translated into practice according to the codes and guidelines a counsellor has contracted to abide by and according to the individual's philosophy of counselling. Codes evolve over time and range in presentation from the detailed and specific to the more general. The codes set out the current consensus on standards to be applied in the practice of members in each association. Issues that are consistent between the associations include adequate training, confidentiality and proper conduct. Reasons for the revision of codes include integrating learning from complaints and ethical dilemmas, changes in legislation and changes in the use of language. Experience also influences how the profession applies the universal moral principles. An important point about codes is that when practitioners belong to more than one professional association they are bound by the most rigorous aspects of each code.

Ethics in practice, therefore, starts with an understanding of the universal moral principles and counselling values and principles, and with a commitment to integrate these into day-to-day practice in every way (see Figure 2).

Practice issues

The following list of issues that a counsellor needs to consider is not exhaustive, but it identifies some aspects of practice that require thoughtful decisions. The examples are more pertinent to some settings than to others. These are issues for counsellors but also apply to other practitioners. Attention to these points can reduce the incidence of ethical dilemmas.

Office accommodation needs to be suitable for the purpose of counselling; there should be privacy of access for clients, adequate soundproofing, security for records, lack of interruption by others in person or by telephone and comfortable furnishings. Rowan (1988) offers some useful guidance on some of the ethical and practice issues on this point. It is usually desirable to have another person present on the premises to ensure safety where there is any risk or threat to the well-being of the counsellor (Syme 1994). The need for suitable premises applies whatever the setting. This is such an important

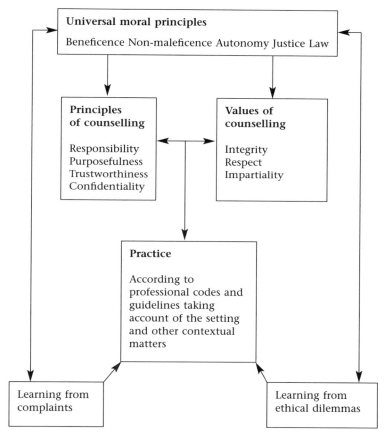

Figure 2   The links between principles, values and practice

question that describing the accommodation where counselling takes place is one of the requirements when applying for BAC individual counsellor accreditation (registration) (BAC 1994).

Advertising and pre-counselling information need to reflect accurately what counsellors are offering. Most professional associations emphasize the importance, for example, of advertising training, qualifications and memberships in ways that conform to acceptable standards (Jones and Syme 1994).

Contingency planning for sudden breaks and endings, in the event of serious illness or an accident, is particularly important as these will have implications for ongoing client work irrespective of the setting. Other sorts of planning include alternative support networks in the event of one's supervisor having to stop working suddenly and access to the supervisor or other experienced practitioners at short notice in the event of a problem. There are other more personal issues to plan for such as financial cover for the independent practitioner when circumstances require a break from work.

Counsellors need to keep a healthy balance between their personal and professional lives and need to know their limits in terms of maximum workloads. Counselling can be a solitary and stressful activity that affects counsellor well-being. There are many restorative routes to good functioning and this must be attended to outside the counselling room. In addition, counsellors need to be aware of their own inner world and of those occasions when client work touches on their own issues and life experiences.

Contracts may be verbal or recorded or a mixture of both. They cover important matters clients need to know about such as fees, limits to confidentiality, ways of working, arrangements for holidays, missed sessions, illness, extra sessions and contact between sessions. Effective contracting establishes and confirms the purposefulness of counselling.

The law relating to the work of counsellors inevitably changes over time. Counsellors are responsible for taking all reasonable steps to be aware of the law as it applies to their practice and can refer to a range of sources such as Jenkins (1997) and Bond (1999). Awareness of legislation that applies more generally is good practice. Particularly relevant are statutes concerning discrimination such as the Rehabilitation of Offenders Act (1974), the Sex Discrimination Act (1973) and Amendments (1986), the Race Relations Act (1976) and the Disability Discrimination Act (1995). Other useful statutes include the Mental Health Acts, Protection from Harassment Act (1997), the Suicide Act (1961), the Children Act (1989) and employment legislation. Recent employment legislation includes the Public Interest Disclosure Act (1998), which offers protection to employees who make a qualifying disclosure of information, in good faith, on certain issues in the public interest, except where the person making the disclosure commits an offence by making it [Section 43 (3)].

It is important for every practitioner to examine those areas of practice that seem most likely to give rise to complaints. This information can usually be found in professional journals. Learning from others is an ongoing contribution to good practice. When practitioners make mistakes, and these inevitably occur, owning up causes the least harm and can assist the process of managing complaints when these instances are reported formally (Casemore 1999). It is good practice for counsellors to have professional liability insurance, and essential in some circumstances such as when working independently.

Aspects of confidentiality are explored in many of the questions in this book. Confidentiality is not only a good practice issue; counsellors who breach an agreement about confidentiality could be sued. Confidentiality is an aspect of the profession that presents many dilemmas. In order to assist its members, BAC has on two occasions sought a barrister's opinion concerning confidentiality. Friel (1998) found that the nature of the counselling relationship is 'fiduciary' in legal terminology, meaning pertaining to a duty akin to that of trustee.

Counsellors need to examine their attitudes to all issues of difference. This can be done in various ways, including asking for feedback from colleagues and clients, monitoring their work, discussion within counselling supervision and by paying attention to the use of language. Concerning race, it is also necessary to understand the relationships between black people and white people today and the historical roots of these relationships, and to understand contemporary society and how power is used and abused (Lago and Thompson 1997). A recommended source is 'The Stephen Lawrence Inquiry' MacPherson of Cluny (1999). Equality issues are present in our work with all clients directly or indirectly and can concern race, ethnic origin, culture, religion, age, class, disability, gender and sexual preferences.

No single counsellor can offer effective help to every client. Paul Watchell (1997b) helpfully describes the distinction between having a good therapeutic relationship with a client and actually being effective as a therapist. An understanding of this clearly links with the ethical principles of purposefulness and the responsibilities of counsellors not to exploit their clients by continuing beyond the point of counselling actually helping.

Ethical counselling requires from the counsellor a philosophy of counselling that encompasses the 'personal and theoretical' and demonstrates 'how it is congruent with your current counselling practice' (BAC 1994: 11 (application form)). Like codes and guidelines, a counsellor's philosophy evolves through experience and learning but can be coherent and in awareness at each stage of development.

Fees, funding and resources are invariably an issue. If the client pays the counsellor directly, what happens if the client's circumstances change midway through the work? When the counsellor is paid by an organization, to what extent is the organization also a client? If the counsellor is working in a voluntary agency, how does the agency manage questions about donations from clients? Do clients value counselling more if they pay fees? Without adequate resources, a counsellor is unable to provide an ethical service: coun-selling premises, advertising, counselling supervision, training and continuing professional development all cost money.

Ethical dilemmas

Ethical dilemmas arise on those occasions when conflicts occur between universal moral principles, counselling values and the ethical principles of counselling in work with clients. Such situations are sometimes difficult to anticipate and therefore may be unex-pected as well as complex and may also be urgent. Bond (1993) and Shillito-Clark (1996) have offered effective strategies for ethical problem-solving and the following model obviously has roots in their work (see Figure 3). The suggestions are for counsellors, but apply to trainers, supervisors and researchers too. It is in the nature of an ethical dilemma that choice be made between alternatives, none of which is entirely satisfactory (Bond 1997).

1 *Understand the problem.* The first step is to set out the problem ver-bally or in writing. The process of describing it can itself point the counsellor in the direction of a resolution. If there is no clear res-olution it assists the counsellor to identify where best to seek help – counselling literature, the supervisor, the professional association for advice, experienced colleagues, the codes and guidelines of other professional associations and so on.

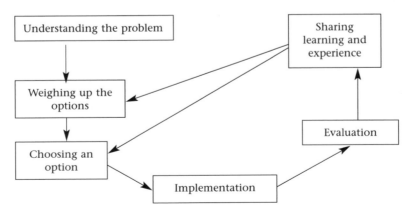

Figure 3   A model for resolving ethical dilemmas

2 *Weigh up the options.* Having done all possible research and thinking, a number of options will present themselves. The counsellor has to decide which is the fairest, which does the most good and least harm, which takes account of the client's autonomy and which is lawful, while considering the counselling values, ethical principles and relevant codes. The setting of the counselling may also have a bearing on the options.

3 *Choose an option.* Counselling supervision is the proper place to discuss and move towards choosing an option. Additionally, the counsellor may wish to talk through the choice with experienced colleagues, to ascertain their views. The counsellor may wish to discuss the dilemma with the client, if this is appropriate, and outline the options, if this is possible, before taking any steps.

4 *Implement the option.* The counsellor takes the necessary action, taking care to ensure that this causes the minimum of harm to the client. Implementation includes thorough discussion, whenever possible, with the client of action taken.

5 *Evaluate the outcome.* The counsellor should try to evaluate the outcome of action taken to resolve a conflict of ethical principles, for future learning. Ideally this is done together with the client and within counselling supervision.

6 *Share learning and experience.* One of the points made by Bond (1993) concerns how counsellors might feel about being judged in public on the way they resolved an ethical dilemma. Sharing learning and experience is one of the tests of the validity of ethical dilemma resolution. This also benefits other practitioners as the learning may influence the next revision of a code.

Conclusion

The aim of this section has been to set the scene for a range of questions concerning ethics in counselling and therapy. Ethical practice clearly begins long before the first client arrives and continues after retirement from practice. Codes are invaluable tools to the daily work of counsellors, yet we never know what today may bring in the shape of a dilemma that no one could possibly foresee. Working according to a code and attending sensitively to the needs of clients, based on a coherent philosophy and careful planning, all contribute to ethical practice.

SECTION 2

Ethics in counselling

Question 1

Ethical counselling is properly described as highly confidential. What are some of the limits to complete confidentiality within a counselling relationship?
Caroline Jones

It is impossible to anticipate what issues or content might arise in any counselling relationship so it is good practice to state, when contracting, that counselling is highly confidential. In certain specific circumstances, confidentiality is limited by statute, or by ethical considerations enshrined in codes and guidelines or by constraints arising from the setting.

The law

There is generally no duty to report a crime but current statutes to note, with the caution that the interpretations of these statutes are those of the author and are not authoritative legal interpretations, are given below.

- The Prevention of Terrorism Act (Temporary Provisions) 1989 [Section 18] makes it an offence to fail, without reasonable excuse, to disclose information as soon as practicable, knowing or believing this to be of material assistance in the prevention or investigation of an act of terrorism connected with the affairs of Northern Ireland.

- The Drug Trafficking Act 1994 [Section 52] makes it an offence not to disclose to a constable as soon as reasonably practicable if one knows or suspects a person is engaged in drug money laundering; it may be an offence to tell the person concerned that this step has been taken.
- The Road Traffic Act 1988 [Section 172] requires any person upon request to provide information in their power to supply to permit identification of the driver of a motor vehicle involved in certain offences.
- The Police and Criminal Evidence Act 1984 [Section 12] requires the police to obtain a warrant from a circuit judge to seize 'excluded materials' such as personal records (see also Question 2). Personal records are classed as 'records which a person has acquired or created in the course of any trade, business, profession or other occupation or for the purposes of any paid or unpaid office and which he holds in confidence [Section 11(a)]. Section 12 further defines personal records as 'documentary and other records concerning an individual (whether living or dead) who can be identified from them and relating to (a) physical and mental health, (b) spiritual counselling or assistance or (c) counselling for the purposes of personal welfare by any voluntary organization or individual'.
- The Criminal Procedure and Investigations Act 1996 introduced a new procedure amending the Criminal Procedure (Attendance of Witnesses) Act 1965. In order to obtain a witness summons or documents the applicant must now show [Section 66] that 'a person is likely to be able to give evidence likely to be material evidence, or produce any document or thing likely to be material evidence for the purpose of any criminal proceedings before the Crown Court' and that 'the person will not voluntarily attend as a witness or will not voluntarily produce the document or thing'. Power to require advance production of documents (under seal) is also part of this amendment. The new Data Protection Act 1998 also has relevance here. This now allows a data subject to request in writing to have access to manual data held on them since October 1998, including any expression of opinion on an individual. This applies to written record cards, files and notes.
- The Health and Safety Executive gives powers to its inspectors under the Health and Safety at Work Act 1974 [Section 20, 2(j)] to require any person, where there is reasonable cause to believe that person is able to give any information relevant to an investigation, to answer questions and sign a written declaration of the truth of

the answers. A constable can be brought along if there is reasonable cause to apprehend any serious obstruction in the execution of these duties [Section 20 2(b)].

Codes and guidelines

These contain the ethical principles of the professional associations. Concerning the law, guidance differs. Some codes require

- adherence to all relevant laws, regulations and guidelines affecting their work (AHPP 1999a: 2.4),
- that counsellors take all reasonable steps to be aware of current law as it applies to their counselling practice (BAC 1997: B.1.6.1),
- awareness of specific legal implications of their work including the general legal requirements concerning giving and withholding information (BPS, DCoP Guidelines 1998: 1.6),
- that counsellors must work within the law (COSCA Statement of Ethics 2.9),

while others make no specific reference to the law.

Codes and guidelines normally include reference both to responsibility and confidentiality. The management of confidentiality is detailed in the fuller codes. Codes and guidelines are particularly helpful for those exceptional occasions where, on balance, in the interests of clients and others it is more responsible for counsellors to have some discretion about confidentiality. Such occasions usually involve weighing universal moral principles one against another. The choices individual counsellors and therapists make, about whether or not to break confidentiality, reflect their own philosophy and the circumstances. Venier (1998) urges the profession to have greater clarity about confidentiality and privacy. Codes also place on record the importance of competence through, in particular, regular supervision and individual monitoring of effectiveness. Supervision is an activity that involves limited breaches of confidentiality (see Section 1). Monitoring effectiveness may involve the recording of sensitive data that, under the Data Protection Act 1998, may only be kept if it is justified as relevant (see Question 28).

Settings

Depending on the setting of the counselling, there may be obligations to assist the Local Authorities or delegated bodies under the provisions of the Children Act 1989 [Section 47 (9) and (11)] unless it would be unreasonable to have to do so. This section concerns the protection of children at risk and the duties of Local Authorities to investigate by seeking assistance and information. Similarly, the Crime and Public Disorder Act 1998 allows the passing of confidential information between agencies in order to protect vulnerable communities from crime and disorder. This legislation creates a power to share (not generally personally identifiable information) but not a duty and may apply in some settings. The identity of clients using the services of the counsellor is also confidential and safeguarding this confidentiality requires planning. The following points, while under specific headings, may be relevant to any counselling relationship irrespective of setting.

Independent practice

In this setting, counsellors have the greatest autonomy about the management of confidentiality in terms of, for example, record-keeping and scheduling appointments so that clients do not cross paths. No information on the identity of clients needs to be shared except where reception staff are employed.

Institutional settings

Counsellors employed by institutions may be contracted to abide by additional limits to confidentiality and need to make these clear to those using the service. It is possible to run these services without compromising the identity of clients although the employment of support staff may limit this.

Agencies

Voluntary and independent agencies should provide written statements on any additional limitations to confidentiality and the counsellors are bound by these and must explain these to clients, including whether the agreement about confidentiality is between the counsellor and the client or the agency and the client. A busy agency is likely to have more than one client in the waiting room at the same time.

Medical settings

Counselling in this sector, where multidisciplinary teams provide care for patients, requires care in negotiating the way counsellors as team members keep client confidentiality. In medicine, the principle of 'continuity of care' requires adequate record-keeping so that in the absence of the regular GP or nurse, for example, another professional can effectively continue to treat a patient. Counselling and therapy differ in that in the absence of the regular counsellor or therapist, the client will either delay further work until that person returns or start afresh with another with a new contract (Hill 1999). It is important that all parties understand this distinction.

Conclusion

Where counsellors consider the limits to confidentiality to be harmful or unhelpful to counselling, they can and have sought assistance from the professional associations. Examples include occasions when the right to privacy while in counselling (Friel 1992) and the right to discretion about maintaining confidentiality over disclosures of abuse by clients under the age of 18 appeared to be under threat (Friel 1998). Ultimately, counsellors may face difficult decisions about their choice of setting if the limits to confidentiality do not fit comfortably with their philosophy of counselling or their personal values. Members of BAC are bound by their code (1997: B.3.3.2) to take responsibility for this aspect of their practice.

Question 2

What should counsellors consider when contacted by persons such as solicitors or the police and other authorities in connection with client work or when clients request such assistance on their behalf?
Caroline Jones

The key responsibilities in these circumstances are to the clients and to the aims and goals of the counselling relationship and responses may vary according to the counsellor's philosophy and codes or guidelines. This question illustrates how counselling is different from other forms of helping (BAC 1991).

A sensible first step is always carefully to reread codes and guidelines and other resources counsellors need to have ready to hand in order to distinguish between those circumstances where there is discretion and those where the counsellor needs to take account of the law. These include the relevant statutes, information from professional associations and other sources (Jenkins 1997; Bond 1999). The setting of the counselling can also dictate the way counsellors may or must respond.

The next step concerns considering the request in the context of the purpose and nature of the particular counselling relationship. These will have been identified at the time of contracting. When the purpose of the counselling is established as therapeutic, then the situation is different from those occasions when a counsellor or therapist is engaged purely for the purpose of assessment with the intention of producing a report. There are occasions when a counsellor can clarify their own position during contracting about what they are prepared to do about providing reports or testimony in court if this sort of request is likely to arise. Making a policy statement in pre-counselling literature is another option.

Whenever solicitors, the police or any other authority approach a counsellor concerning a client, the counselling relationship is affected and the purpose and nature of the work interrupted by the intrusion of an outside element. This applies whether or not the client wishes the counsellor to take some action with their express consent and whether or not the counsellor is willing to do so. Sometimes the counsellor may receive a letter from a solicitor, for example, seeking information. Clearly, the client has given the counsellor's details to the solicitor and if this has occurred without prior knowledge or agreement, this in itself needs discussion that interrupts the counselling process. The client's initial view that the counsellor responding to their solicitor, for example, will be helpful to them and be in their best interests, needs very careful exploration. It is the responsibility of the counsellor to clarify the potential consequences of taking such action on behalf of the client, such as how the information may be used by others and how it may be stored and accessed by other parties, thus further diminishing confidentiality.

Counsellors also have the responsibility to decline to do what is asked of them if they consider it to be harmful to the counselling or not in the best interests of the client. This will be difficult when counsellor and client disagree. Refusing the request may trigger a premature end to the counselling relationship but complying does not guarantee an appropriate ending. A sensible precaution, when counsellors do agree to such requests, is to draw up a 'waiver of confidentiality' that both counsellor and client sign.

Timing is an important factor on these occasions. When a counsellor is asked to produce a report for a solicitor part-way through the counselling contract, the counsellor needs to consider whether information might be disclosed later on which might have led them to make a different decision or to have written a different report. On the occasions that a counsellor agrees voluntarily to be a witness, consideration is required on how this decision will affect the timing and management of the ending of the counselling contract, and the form in which the counsellor keeps case-notes.

Articles helpful to counsellors facing these circumstances have been published, and include Littlehailes (1998) and Scoggins, Litton and Palmer (1997). These offer personal accounts of assisting clients outside the counselling room and discuss some of the resulting consequences. An article on the especially important, bearing in mind the subsequent requirements of the Data Protection Act 1998, issue of case-notes has appeared in the *Psychologist* (Jakobi and Pratt 1992). Additionally, accounts of the actions of Hayman are outlined in various sources (Bond 1993; Jenkins 1997; Venier 1998).

Counsellors need to consider their legal obligations. While offering some brief guidance on this point I wish to add the proviso that counsellors should seek legal advice, should contact their professional insurers, their professional association(s), supervisor and other experienced practitioners whenever they feel unsure about any steps they wish to take.

Solicitors

When counsellors receive a request from a solicitor, there is

- no obligation to answer the enquiry,
- no obligation to make a statement for the purpose of legal proceedings,
- no obligation to attend court at the request of parties involved in the case and
- no obligation to attend at the request of lawyers.

When counsellors decide not to assist, it is good practice to state this in writing. When counsellors agree to any requests, other aspects to consider are how time-consuming this will be and how their time spent on this is to be reimbursed – an issue irrespective of setting.

Counsellors need not be persuaded to cooperate under the threat that otherwise a subpoena or witness summons will be issued. The Criminal Procedure and Investigations Act 1996 requires that a witness summons or documents must be material to the case, that applications to the court are necessary for a witness to be summonsed or information subpoenaed and that it is for the judge to decide these issues at a preparatory hearing or pre-trial hearing. Again, an issue to consider at this point is timing. After voluntarily producing a report, or agreeing to be a witness, counsellors may be in a difficult position regarding confidentiality if subsequently clients disclose information that they prefer not to have revealed in court or in writing. This could put counsellors in the position of having produced a report that they later know to be misleading, causing a dilemma over integrity, or of holding information that they may be obliged to reveal under cross-examination. The time gap between agreeing to be a witness and the case coming to court is entirely outside the control of the counsellor or the client. The timing of a preparatory hearing is more likely to be when the case is imminent. Being summonsed to appear indicates that there are compelling professional reasons for not volunteering to be in court. Counsellors must obey a witness summons and at this point seeking legal advice is strongly recommended.

Criminal Injuries Compensation Authority (CICA)

When counsellors are approached by the CICA, usually for a confidential report to assist the Authority in assessing the psychological element of a claim for compensation, they can choose how fully they respond. This can be as brief as a confirmation that counselling is taking or has taken place, along the lines of 'x has been in counselling with y for n number of sessions, since . . .', or a fuller response. When clients undertake counselling for help to recover from post-traumatic stress occasioned by crime, the possibility that the CICA might request information is a matter that can be discussed during contracting and with reference to pre-counselling literature where policy is explicitly stated. Alternatively, counsellors may reasonably anticipate this eventuality, and if it is their normal practice to assist in these circumstances, discussion about the content of the report can be deferred until a request is received. The client should be given a full draft before it is submitted, for the purpose of gaining their express consent, again in writing. The CICA currently offers counsellors a fee for this service with the aim of obtaining from a professional an objective and independent assessment that modifies or corroborates the victim's own statements and offers a prognosis.

The CICA considers that restricting the report to confirmation that counselling has occurred would not necessarily affect the outcome of a claim if the relevant information was obtainable from other sources but that such a statement on its own would not be helpful to them (CICA, personal communication). Conditions ranging from shock and temporary mental anxiety that are medically confirmed, to disabling mental disorder confirmed by psychiatric diagnosis, attract compensation (CICA 1999).

Police

There is normally no obligation to answer enquiries or hand over any kind of document (which may be turned into a statement) or sign any document when approached by the police, although a counsellor choosing to do so must answer any questions truthfully. Exceptions are identified in Question 1. Very occasionally, a counsellor may consider answering police enquiries in the public interest. Such circumstances involve the counsellor in a serious ethical and moral dilemma. Ideally, the counsellor will be able to ask for time to obtain legal advice, and to seek help from their supervisor and other experienced practitioners, as well as contact their professional insurers for more practical support. Most importantly, the counsellor needs time to contact the client for their consent to break confidentiality or at least to inform him or her of the course of action to be taken, although in certain circumstances it may be an offence to do so (see Question 1).

The courts

If summonsed as a witness, the counsellor will want to try to limit the breaking of confidentiality to those matters strictly relevant to the case and can seek the assistance of the judge. This includes ensuring that the judge is instructing the counsellor to answer the questions put, thus making any breaking of confidentiality defensible in law. Clients need reminding that when under cross-examination, counsellors could be required to answer questions on any aspect of the counselling the court allows is relevant to the case. Counsellors who foresee that they might wish to decline to answer questions are advised to have their own legal representation.

Inquests and the work of coroners (England and Wales)

Coroners hold inquests when a death is not due to natural causes in order to establish the circumstances (Home Office 1996). Many inquests are held without a jury but when a death has occurred in prison or in police custody or if the death resulted from an incident at work, the inquest is held with a jury, who make the final decision. The coroner decides whom to call as witnesses and anyone with 'a proper interest' may question the witnesses either directly or by having a lawyer ask questions on their behalf. A witness may either be asked to attend or may receive a formal summons to do so. Counsellors may wish to consult beforehand with either the coroner or the coroner's officers to reaffirm that the confidentiality of the counselling relationship extends beyond the death of clients. The coroner determines the relevance of questioning in court and makes every effort to limit upset to people's private lives unless this is unavoidable in the interests of justice.

Fatal accident inquiries and the work of the Procurator Fiscal (Scotland)

The Procurator Fiscal arranges for a fatal accident inquiry (FAI) when a person dies as a result of an accident at work or in custody or if the death was sudden, suspicious or unexplained or occurred in circumstances which give rise to serious public concern. The FAI is arranged by the Procurator Fiscal, who notifies interested parties. It is held in a local sheriff court and is presided over by the sheriff. Witnesses are examined by the Procurator Fiscal and can be questioned by relatives or a solicitor representing them (Scottish Office 1998).

Finally, some counsellors may be requested to produce reports by those with whom they have contractual obligations. For example, managers or personnel officers or medical staff in occupational health services may seek reports from workplace counsellors or those working for employee assistance programmes. Counsellors in these circumstances should consider whether producing such reports fits with their philosophy and whether speaking on behalf of the client is necessary or appropriate. Again, when clients in this setting request reports or when reports are likely to be requested, this interrupts and influences the process and purpose of counselling.

Question 3

What are the ethical issues to consider when a client offers a gift?
Caroline Jones

For the purposes of this question a 'gift' is defined in a wide-ranging way to include items of significant monetary or sentimental value, including the offer of a legacy. This question requires consideration on each occasion that it arises, in order to determine the meaning and significance of the offer. There is a clear conflict between the client's autonomy, on the occasions that a client chooses to offer a gift, and the counselling ethical principles of trustworthiness and responsibility. The counsellor has to decide what does the most good and least harm to the client, whether the values of counselling could be compromised and how accepting or not accepting fits with their philosophy of counselling.

This question is difficult whatever the setting. In independent practice the client may see no difference between paying for the sessions, as contracted, and adding a gift as an additional gesture of gratitude. In the voluntary sector, the client may consider that the donations given per session belong to the agency and wish to offer something more personal to the counsellor. In an institutional setting, the client knows that they do not pay a fee or donation directly and again may wish to offer something more personal to the counsellor.

The counsellor has the opportunity to remind the client of the contract and boundaries they agreed at the start and the purpose of the relationship – to explore and achieve therapeutic aims and goals. This may be a timely reminder for a client that has been in counselling for a while and is experiencing warmth, attention and interest from the counsellor. It may also be a useful reminder for the counsellor that the experience of counselling can be powerful for clients, prompting a wish to offer something of value in return. The timing may be significant, especially if the issue of endings is on the agenda. There might be other motives for the offer of a gift. Perhaps the client is testing how far to trust the counsellor within the counselling relationship or more generally testing the counsellor's integrity (Fong and Cox 1997). Alternatively, for some clients there may be an issue of wanting to be special and wishing to be remembered or feeling that they are valued only through their gifts to others. Another possible motive may be to address the power imbalance that exists in the counselling relationship. The possibilities, together with the factor of the meaning of the offer from a theoretical perspective, especially if there is a symbolic meaning to the gift, can be explored both with the client and within counselling supervision. There may be gender, cultural or other issues influencing some clients or it could be simply that the client has a generous personality and is expressing it within this relationship in the same way as in other areas of life.

While the issue of gifts can be managed when in the open, it is important to remember that the counsellor may be receiving favours without necessarily being aware that this is happening. A client may be in a position of influence to refer others to the counsellor. Counsellors in any setting are aware that new clients often make contact having heard through the grapevine that a particular counsellor is effective. It would obviously be exploitative for a counsellor to ask clients to recommend them to others, but we cannot prevent it from happening.

There is also a dilemma facing a counsellor when clients unexpectedly bring gifts to sessions, such as a 'thank you' card, a card marking a religious festival, a cream-cake or a bunch of flowers. At a final session, this may be the client's way of signalling acceptance of the ending of the active phase of counselling and that to accept them is a mark of respect. When the gift is in the form of an invitation to a social occasion such as a wedding party or retirement party, however, this might signal that caution is required as the client may be exploring the possibility of a subsequent social relationship. This is discussed in more detail in Question 6.

Before accepting an offer of a significant gift, counsellors may want to take the sensible precaution of discussing this with their supervisor and perhaps their professional association(s) (Bond 1993). Finally, very occasionally, counsellors may feel the impulse to offer a client a gift. This would certainly be an issue that requires exploration in counselling supervision. BASRT (1999: 1.6) explicitly recommends that the giving of favours or substantial gifts on either side should be avoided.

Question 4

What are my responsibilities when a client's actions or behaviour puts others at risk or when a client is at risk from the behaviour of others?
Carol Shillito-Clarke

The ethical question which underlies these two situations is: at what point does respect for the client's autonomy become secondary to the need to intervene to protect them, or others, from harm? In working with issues of risk the therapist has to accept a number of responsibilities. These include

- promoting the client's autonomy and sense of social responsibility,
- fulfilling their duty of care to the client and to those affected by the client's actions,
- being aware of their own values, beliefs and feelings and how these might affect their decisions,
- ensuring that all contractual obligations are made clear to the client,
- clarifying and assessing the nature and degree of risk,
- managing the process with respect for the client and themselves and
- consulting with a supervisor and other appropriate professionals at all stages.

The client's autonomy versus the therapist's duty of care

The ethical principle of autonomy values the freedom of the individual to make their own choices and to decide their own actions. According to the BAC *Code of Ethics and Practice for Counsellors* (1997), one of the aims of all forms of therapy is to help the client to develop and enact their own decision-making processes according to their own beliefs and value systems. Therefore the counsellor does not normally give advice to or act on behalf of their clients and must respect their confidentiality (BAC 1997). This suggests that the principal role of the counsellor is to observe, reflect and question rather than 'do something' for the client.

However, the concept of autonomy does not imply unlimited freedom for the individual to do as they please; it is tempered by respect for the autonomy of others. Therefore, in order to be truly autonomous in making an informed decision about a life course, the client needs to be aware, and take account, of the autonomous needs of others (Holmes and Lindley 1989; Bond 1993; Gordon 1999). It may be argued that, as the only representative of 'others' in the therapy session, the therapist has a responsibility to present the possible needs of others to the client while maintaining integrity, impartiality and respect for the client's position.

Every therapist has a 'duty of care' towards a client and is responsible for their safety during the session (BAC 1997). A dilemma arises when 'doing nothing' may be unethical in a situation where action and the breaching of confidentiality by the therapist is necessary to prevent harm to or by the client. 'In such circumstance, *someone's* autonomy must be compromised, and, given that [the patient] has already repudiated respect for her intended victim's autonomy, it might be wrong for the therapist to sacrifice the innocent victim to protect [the patient]' (Holmes and Lindley 1989: 184). Francis (1999) suggests that while the principle of 'do no harm' should usually take precedence over other ethical principles, its precedence should not be considered an absolute rule.

The therapist's awareness of their own feelings

It is important to note that this question specifies actions and behaviours rather than thoughts and intentions. For the therapist, there is a significant difference. The therapeutic relationship is one in which the client can openly explore feelings, thoughts, ideas, fantasies and the meaning and consequences of actions without having to act them out. In doing so, client and therapist may experience and need to contain strong emotional energies such as fear, anger and anxiety. The therapist must be aware of how these processes interact with their personal experiences of dealing with anger in others and in themselves, and their own theoretical, moral, cultural and perhaps religious beliefs. The temptation to make a premature disclosure or to deny the seriousness of the situation must be resisted.

The therapist's contractual obligations

As a situation involving risk may arise without warning, the therapist needs to have already thought through their own possible reactions to the threat of harm, their contractual obligations to the client and any employing organization and their options for working therapeutically. Francis (1999: 112) points out that 'under stress there is a tendency to restrict consideration of available choices and to review them in an unsystematic manner'.

Any limits imposed by the therapist or the setting on the client's right to confidentiality need to be made clear as part of the initial contract (BAC 1997). Additionally, therapists who work for an organization, institution or agency need to be clear about the relevant policies and procedures relating to risk and to breaches of confidentiality.

Further issues are raised if there is a question about the client's competence to make informed decisions because of age, mental ability or other impairment whether temporary or permanent. The client whose competence becomes impaired during the course of therapy, perhaps through illness, accident or the effect of drugs (whether prescribed or illegal), needs careful consideration in supervision. Consultation with the client's medical advisor may be particularly important, preferably with the client's permission.

Assessment of risk

It is part of a therapist's responsibilities to assess the reality and severity of any risk of harm, either to the client or to others, which becomes apparent during therapy. The therapist's theoretical orientation will largely determine how this is done. The more information that can be gathered, the better will be the therapist's understanding of the level of risk and the degree of urgency with which the situation needs to be dealt. The same will be true for anyone else with whom the information may have to be shared in consultation. A process of sensitive and focused enquiry may be important for the client too, emphasizing the seriousness with which he or she is being taken and helping them to clarify their own position.

Working with the client who is angry

If a client is threatening, or disclosing actions and behaviour that put another person or persons at risk, it can be difficult for the therapist to maintain a position of respect and impartiality. It is, however, important to proceed calmly and firmly, to clarify what is actually happening and to consider fully, with the client, the options and their consequences.

The therapist has a responsibility to keep both client and self safe from physical harm during the session (BAC 1997). Therapists should be familiar with anger-management techniques, some of which may appear to contradict theoretical training. For example, a client who is very angry may misperceive impassive, reflective or interpretative interventions and become more emotionally aroused rather than less.

Working with the client who is at risk from another

The role of the therapist is to empower the client's autonomy and to help them to evaluate the situation objectively and consider alternative courses of action. In high-risk situations, for example when the client has already been attacked by a partner, it may be necessary to be more directive in order to access the help of external sources of support and inform the appropriate authorities.

In every case, the therapist must be very clear about the difference between counselling, giving advice and information and taking direct action. Before rushing to intervene, she or he needs to consider the whole situation, including who else might know about it and perhaps already be involved. It may be that there are other people or services that would be able to act more appropriately for or on behalf of the client, particularly if under-age children are also involved. It is ethically important to hold firm therapeutic boundaries in the client's best interest. Resisting action that alters the therapeutic boundaries may be more beneficial to the client in the long run.

Supervision and consultancy

In cases where the therapist has good reason to believe that there is a serious risk of harm, either to the client or to someone else, consideration of the case in supervision is essential. Informing other appropriate authorities, such as the client's GP and the line-manager, may also be important. The need to breach confidentiality should be explained clearly to the client, and, where possible, their consent should be gained. Any disclosure of confidential information should be 'restricted to relevant information and conveyed only to appropriate people and for appropriate reasons likely to alleviate the exceptional circumstances' (BAC 1997: B.3.4.2). The case should be clearly documented at all stages.

Holding the balance between maintaining the client's confidentiality and their right to autonomy and avoiding harm for the client or others can be delicate and stressful processes for any counsellor. The situation is not one that should be faced alone.

Question 5

How can I ensure I am aware of my prejudices and minimize their effect on my counselling relationships?
Roger Casemore

The very nature of human development through imitation and assimilation predicates that we will acquire opinions and biases from those with whom we are in contact while we grow up. As we develop through childhood and adolescence into adulthood, we acquire values and beliefs about ourselves and about other people. We develop these values in order to help us to determine the kind of person we should be and what we should or should not do. Many of these values are introjected into us at an unconscious level by our parents, families, teachers and religious leaders and by society in general through education and through the various forms of the media. These introjected values produce attitudes in us, including preconceived opinions or biased views, in favour of or against almost anything you can think of but most particularly in relation to other people who are in some way different from us. Rooted in our primitive, atavistic memory is the knowledge that in order for each of us to survive and succeed in our own individual small world, we have to strive to be as alike as possible to the significant other people who also populate our small world. Through that process we acquire beliefs, views and opinions that are not based on evidence and can quite often be completely irrational or illogical, ill informed and rooted in ignorance.

As we mature and grow older, we also deliberately choose to acquire other values on the basis of our experience of people and of life. These values are most often (but not always) acquired unconsciously and are more likely to be based on the evidence of our experience and knowledge. Both these sets of values lead inescapably to the various prejudices we develop.

It is essential to recognize that none of us can be entirely free of prejudice and that, indeed, many of the prejudices we hold are important if not essential to our survival and our success. Similarly, as human beings we need to have the capacity to discriminate, to be able to make choices and to be able to act on the basis of differences. Discrimination in itself is an essential human capacity, without which we could not cope or survive in a hostile environment or succeed in a supportive one. However, when discrimination occurs as a result of prejudice, which is irrational, illogical or ill informed, it can be exceedingly dangerous, causing emotional, physical, social or economic harm to individuals, groups, communities and even nationalities; it can also be harmful to the person who is discriminating.

In choosing to be a counsellor, I am clearly discriminating in what I choose to be. I may also discriminate in choosing the approach I wish to use, where I wish to work and the clients I choose to work with. All of these choices should be made in an informed way but there is no doubt that my introjected values and prejudices will play some part in those choices and that in joining the counselling world I will also develop some new acquired values both consciously and unconsciously. Along with these new values will grow the capacity to discriminate in this field of my experience and to act with prejudice both appropriately and inappropriately.

Carl Rogers believed that there were six core conditions essential for therapy to be effective. The fourth of these conditions was that 'the counsellor experiences unconditional positive regard for the client' (Rogers 1957). This means the counsellor being fully accepting of the other person, treating them with non-possessive warmth – prizing the other individual and having a non-judgemental attitude towards them, and that the client to some degree experiences the counsellor valuing them in that way. As a person-centred counsellor I am committed to that principle of offering my clients unconditional positive regard, accepting them as of equal value to me, while not necessarily unconditionally accepting everything that they do. If I am to be authentic in this it seems to me to be critically important that I am readily aware of my prejudices and of my capacity for inappropriate prejudicial discriminations so that these do not negatively affect the therapeutic relationships I have with my clients.

Like Schon (1973), I believe that human beings, like all organisms, have a natural tendency to aim for homeostasis – to want to remain in a stable state. I also believe, with Maslow (1954), that human beings have an innate tendency to want to self-actualize and that these two drives are in direct conflict with each other. A consequence of this conflict is that change in human beings is an enormously difficult process. So trying to become aware of and to change my prejudices will take some real effort and commitment and I am unlikely to be able to achieve everything I want to on my own. If I discover within me attitudes and values, prejudices and discriminations that are inappropriate in the work that I do, then it is likely that I will actively resist changing these, no matter how much I want to improve myself. At an unconscious level, I will strive to stay just the way I am (something we all experience in the most frustrating way in our clients). It may mean changing my beliefs about who I am, about the kind of person I should be and about the kinds of things I should and should not do. Becoming aware of my prejudices will not change them and may in fact serve only to reinforce them.

Becoming aware of my prejudices is not like developing a skill or an aptitude, which I may be able to do through training. It is about working on something which is a deeply rooted, integral part of me and a part of my self-concept. Perhaps the first thing I need to do is to make a strong personal commitment to reviewing and monitoring the prejudices which I have and seeking feedback from those who know me well, asking them to identify which prejudices of mine they experience. Taking time to think through and identify my prejudices and to consider which ones are appropriate and which are not would be a useful starting point, particularly if I can check out my perceptions with those of other people whom I trust.

Taking this issue to personal therapy is clearly another useful strategy which I can adopt. I am a strong believer in using personal therapy as a continuing personal development tool, as well as for dealing with crises in my life. I choose to spend some time each year in therapy, for the purpose of ensuring my continuing growth and development as well as reminding me what it feels like to be a client. This seems to me to be an ideal place for me to seek help in identifying and challenging my prejudices with someone who is offering me unconditional positive regard, particularly if they are also working on the awareness of their own prejudices.

Careful monitoring and review of my client work are also clearly essential to identifying where my prejudices may be emerging and where they may be unhelpful. Regular supervision of my casework is clearly the most important vehicle for this, particularly if I can from time to time explicitly ask my supervisor to help me pay attention to my prejudices. It can be most useful to maintain the student habit of writing case studies and to look at these in some depth to see, through my use of language, how my prejudices show through, particularly if I can ask my supervisor or a trusted colleague to read them and to comment on that aspect.

With my clients I work hard to establish a relationship in which they can feel free to give me feedback on how they experience me and my effectiveness as a therapist. I had a shock recently when one of my clients fed back to me surprise at my prejudice against teachers. The client was right, of course, in that I do have a prejudice against poor teachers, although I thought that I worked hard on not letting that spill across to include all teachers. However, my client had noticed my non-verbal and sub-vocal responses when they had been talking about their experience with teachers and had been surprised by those indicators of my wider prejudice. Fortunately, because the relationship between us was one in which the client could feed that back to me, it helped rather than hindered the work we were doing. It also gave me something important to take to supervision and to reflect on further in my daily life.

If many of my prejudices are rooted in ignorance or lack of understanding, then this leads to another strategy which I can adopt. While I can not know everything there is to know about other people's differences, I can make some effort to educate myself to get some understanding of the nature of some of the differences which are likely to affect me. Some of this can be done through training courses, some through reading and private study and some through making the effort to get to know people who are different to me in significant ways. I need to work consistently at being able to appropriately value differences in other people, whatever that difference may be, throughout my life, so that it is an integrated part of me in my work as a therapist.

It seems to me that the prejudices which I have are prejudices which I have throughout the whole of my life. They are rarely, if ever, limited just to appearing in my counselling work. Therefore it is in my wider life that I must examine them and scrutinize them for their appropriateness. I must work hard to uncover those prejudices which are based in ignorance, fear or irrational feelings, which cause me to behave in ways which will affect my relationships with my clients. At the same time, I do not want to get into theequivalent of meaning-less political correctness, by modifying my behaviours, my language and what I say when my attitudes and values have not really changed and my prejudices are merely hidden. Because of our propensity to resist change and to remain in a stable state, old prejudices can reassert themselves without being noticed. Because of our need to be liked and to be valued for being like others whom we like or respect, new prejudices can be acquired subtly and quite unconsciously. Therefore constant vigilance seems to be essential along with a preparedness to seek feedback and help from my friends and colleagues, my supervisor, mypersonal therapist and my clients.

Question 6

Are there any occasions when it is acceptable for a counsellor to have a friendship and/or a sexual relationship with a former client?
Caroline Jones

This is a question where the codes of the professional associations offer guidance ranging from clear instructions to considered discretion (see Figure 4). I will explore points requiring reflection, making no distinctions necessarily between whether it is the counsellor or the client who initiates the suggestion that, after counselling, a friendship or sexual relationship could evolve, as either way the counsellor holds ultimate responsibility. The nature of friendships and sexual relationships needs brief consideration. Friendships can vary between casual and close. Sexual relationships, while intimate at the obvious level, can also be casual or form a part of more loving and close relationships. Counsellors know the harm caused by abusive relationships of any kind, as this is a regular theme in the content of work with clients. They hold the responsibility, on any occasions that post-counselling relationships evolve, for these not to be abusive or cause harm to former clients.

This question provides an example of how and why codes evolve, seen through a brief history of BAC's position on this issue. In 1984 the code stated that 'counsellors are responsible for setting and monitoring the boundaries between a working relationship and friendship, and for making the boundaries as explicit as possible to the client' (BAC 1984: 2.4). This code prohibited sexual activity with clients (BAC 1984: 2.7). In 1990 the code was extensively revised, and the equivalent clauses were worded slightly differently. Clause B.2.2.5

BAC 1997	UKCP 1998	BASRT 1996 (reviewed 1999)	AHPP 1999	COCSA 1996
Counsellors are responsible and must exercise caution. Sexual relationships are prohibited in some circumstances. Counsellors must bring these issues to supervision.	Care is required not to exploit current or past clients in any way.	Counsellors must maintain appropriate boundaries during and after therapy. A sexual relationship with a current or former client is unacceptable.	Sexual intimacies with former clients are prohibited; non-professional relationships with former clients is to be avoided whenever possible.	Avoidance of exploitation extends beyond the termination of the working relationship

Figure 4 Comparisons between codes of some professional associations concerning relationships with former clients

stated that 'counsellors are responsible for setting and monitoring boundaries between the counselling relationship and *any other kind of relationship*, and making this explicit to the client' (my emphasis). Clause B.2.2.6 stated that 'counsellors must not exploit their clients financially, sexually, emotionally or in any other way. Engaging in sexual activity with the client is unethical'. Subsequently, the association recognized that this allowed a loophole for the unscrupulous counsellor, who could end the counselling relationship and immediately start a sexual one. This led to the amendment to the code in 1992 which stated that engaging in sexual activity with former clients within 12 weeks of the ending of counselling was unethical and that a longer prohibition or total ban may be appropriate with some clients. This was not accepted as a long-term statement of ethical practice, and the following year a new subsection to the code (BAC 1993: B.2.3) 'To former clients' was added, replacing the changes made in 1992. The principles established here concerned the counsellor's responsibility for any kind of relationship with a former client, the exercise of caution and discussion within counselling supervision.

No dilemma exists for counsellors who always avoid any sort of post-counselling relationship with clients. Dilemmas exist, however, for counsellors who normally would not consider having a new relationship of any nature with a former client but who might wish to make an occasional exception. If this question arises regularly for counsellors they need to examine their philosophy and practice very thoroughly.

Before exploring some of the many practice issues that are relevant, a counsellor will reflect on what does the most good and least harm in this situation. There is a need to weigh respect for the autonomy of the client who chooses to propose a change in relationship against one's responsibilities as a counsellor to maintain clear boundaries. If it is the counsellor who initiates the change in relationship, consideration is necessary over whether this might pressure a client into a course of action not otherwise sought. Occasionally this question may arise after a significant period of time has elapsed between the ending of counselling and unplanned and unexpected contact between counsellor and former client.

Where counsellors have some flexibility allowed by their codes or guidelines the practice issues can be complex and varied owing to the nature and purpose of counselling, including

- the setting,
- the theoretical approach,
- the content and process of the counselling,
- the length of time of the counselling,
- the intensity of the counselling,
- how the ending was managed and
- the views of the counselling supervisor and other experienced practitioners.

The setting

This has relevance because in some institutional or agency settings there are internal codes of conduct for counsellors prescribing policy on this question. An independent practitioner has more discretion in these matters.

Theoretical approach

The theoretical approach used by the counsellor within this particular counselling relationship is especially significant. Whether working psychodynamically or not, the issues of transference and counter-transference may have arisen and may still require resolution. Clients of a person-centred therapist can confuse the experience of the conditions for the therapeutic process (Rogers 1957) as friend-ship. Similarly, clients experiencing the warmth and immediacy of a gestalt therapist may see these as friendship.

Content and process

With reference to the content and process of counselling, certain issues and experiences within the relationship normally contra-indicate the appropriateness of any other kind of relationship once the counselling has ended. Issues such as loss, bereavement and in particular childhood abuse normally require especially firm bound-aries and containment. Any contact subsequent to the ending of counselling could undo some of the benefits of the therapy and also constitute abuse of the client. Experiences within the therapeutic relationship, such as counsellor self-disclosure, and other indicators that clients pick up, such as the furnishings and decorations in the counselling room, have significance. Some counsellors consider that self-disclosure during counselling can help a client and may do this occasionally or regularly. This practice is flagged by POPAN (see Appendix 3 for complete list) as one of the warning signs of a profes-sional crossing boundaries (1998). The furnishings of a counsellor's room can also offer clues to clients about a counsellor's interests and personality. These may be contributory factors influencing a client towards suggesting a post-counselling relationship. An example of this is where a counsellor has demonstrated an obvious interest in a par-ticular artist by the artwork on the walls of the counselling room. If the counsellor then meets the client at an exhibition of that artist after the counselling has ended, can that be judged as accidental or planned?

Length of counselling contract

The duration of the counselling relationship may be a factor. Ending long-term work can evoke feelings of sadness for both counsellor and client. To fudge this by agreeing to stay in contact in another kind of relationship hinders the completion of counselling.

Intensity

The intensity of the counselling will be another factor to consider. Sometimes a single session and short-term work can be very intense.

Counsellors would need to consider whether a subsequent relationship would reduce the impact of that intensity and lessen the benefits of the therapy.

Management of endings

Where the client has been reluctant to end, it seems to add confusion by agreeing to any sort of post-counselling contact. An 'open door' ending indicates a counsellor's willingness to work again with the client, an offer that would not be possible if any kind of post-counselling relationship develops.

Views of the supervisor and other experienced practitioners

Whether or not the counsellor's code suggests it, taking this issue to counselling supervision is a sensible precaution. The supervisor can assist in identifying avoidable pitfalls and discussing all ethical and practice issues in the context of the work undertaken with this former client. Discussing the question with other experienced practitioners offers a wider range of perspectives. Members of AHPP are obliged to refer this question to the AHPP Ethical Review Procedure (1999b), which adjudicates on proposed courses of action such as 'the desire to progress from a working relationship with a client ... to a non-professional, friendly or intimate relationship'.

Having considered some of the practice issues, a counsellor would also need to consider again whether having a post-counselling relationship of any kind with a former client fits with the values and ethical principles of counselling. The client came originally with a purpose and goals and with the intention of working towards these with someone outside their normal circle of family and friends. This is one of the reasons counsellors do not take friends or family members as clients and is the most persuasive reason why it is sensible to return to the status quo before counselling. It remains the counsellor's responsibility to end the counselling in ways that allow the client to continue to feel safe and contained. Time is often needed after the counselling for clients to internalize the learning they have achieved and this process may be hampered by any kind of subsequent contact.

Having considered all these points, if a counsellor decides to make the transition from the role of counsellor to that of friend or sexual partner, what other questions remain?

- How do you deal with the confidentiality issue, both on an ongoing basis and bearing in mind that responsibility for confidentiality continues after the counselling has ended?
- What time gap is appropriate before the friendship or sexual relationship starts?
- How will this relationship be introduced into the counsellor's existing network of family and friends?
- What if the new relationship ends badly?
- Is this a rare dilemma and, if so, why with this particular client?
- Is this a regular dilemma for you and, if so, are you examining why this happens regularly?
- How can the transition be managed?

Question 7

How do I know that I am working within the limits of my competence?
Gabrielle Syme

A practitioner's competence is considered to be so important that it features in the codes of ethics and practice of BAC, the *Code of Ethics* of UKCP and both the *Code of Conduct* and the *Guidelines for the Practice of Counselling Psychology* of BPS. While the wording differs, all three put the onus on practitioners to maintain and develop their competence. The BAC codes (for counsellors, trainers and supervisors) are unique in being explicit about working within the limits of one's competence and naming the necessity of counselling supervision. Both BAC and BPS then elaborate specific behaviour required of a competent practitioner. How to ensure one's competence as a counsellor is then elaborated in BAC's *Code of Ethics and Practice for Counsellors* (1997), with seven clauses, under the broad heading of competence, outlining good practice (BAC 1997: B.6.1.1–6.1.7), with additional clauses about counsellor safety (B.6.2.1) and counselling supervision (B.6.3.1–6.3.3). The BPS *Code of Conduct* details of the requirements for a competent (counselling) psychologist are laid out in five clauses (BPS 1998: 2.1–2.5). The BPS Division of Counselling Psychology *Guidelines* (1998) Section 2 covers the requirement for supervision. The areas covered under counsellor competence in these codes can be summarized as

- having adequate training and not practising in areas or specialities in which one is not competent,
- not making false claims about ones qualifications or competence, nor allowing others to do so,
- ensuring continuing professional development,
- being willing to receive feedback on competence,
- having self-awareness of physical and emotional state,
- being able to assess one's own competence and refer clients when their needs are outside one's competence,
- having professional indemnity insurance if necessary,
- being willing to consult experienced colleagues and one's supervisor if in an ethical dilemma, and
- taking all reasonable steps to ensure that colleagues for whom one is responsible comply with the requirements of the association (BPS) to work competently.

BAC also has codes of ethics and practice for trainers and supervisors – assurances of competence as a supervisor are outlined in B.2.1 to B.2.6 of the *Code for Supervisors of Counsellors* (BAC 1995) and as a trainer in B.2.1 to B.2.4 of the code for trainers (BAC 1996b). As there is considerable overlap it can be assumed that where counsellor is mentioned it is equally true for a counsellor functioning as a supervisor or trainer.

An in-built assumption of all these clauses on competence is that the counsellor has considerable self-awareness, self-knowledge, ability to self-question, self-honesty and adequate supervision and is open to the judgement of others (clients, colleagues, friends and supervisors) about their performance. If the counsellor's judgement was impaired by alcohol or drugs or due to mental illness, this might not be the case. They might be unable to 'monitor' themselves (BAC 1997: B.6.1.3) and make the necessary decision that they were no longer competent to practice. In this situation the decision would have to be made for them by their supervisor or colleagues, who would be greatly assisted if they were backed up by their professional association. Some professional bodies such as the GMC and UKCC do have 'fitness to practice' or health committees for doctors and nurses respectively, which intervene to prevent a member practising where their functioning is impaired. Both BAC and UKCP are considering the necessity of introducing such a committee. It is considered to be essential for statutory registration.

Competence could be impaired owing to insufficient initial training or not maintaining continuing professional development by not attending further training sessions (BAC 1997: B.6.1.1). A result of this might be incompetence demonstrated by not recognizing the need to refer a client (BAC 1997: B.6.1.4), nor knowing of local referral resources.

All professional counselling and psychotherapy associations identify a minimum quantity of training to ensure competence. If a counsellor is not a member of such a professional body they should ensure that they reach the minimum level, prescribed by one of these associations, of theoretical training, counselling skills training, supervised counselling practice and personal awareness training. In its counsellor-accreditation scheme, BAC identifies the level of training necessary for a mature practitioner; included in this is 40 hours of personal therapy or an equivalent experience. UKCP and BCP demand considerably more hours of therapy. This is an attempt to ensure, but can never guarantee, a level of self-awareness and self-knowledge in a practitioner such that they can assess their own competence.

Most counselling and therapy associations also demand a commitment to continuing professional development but do not stipulate either the quantity, unlike some other professions (such as nursing), or the courses. Clearly this is essential for the revision of skills, time to reflect on skills and the acquisition of new skills and knowledge (particularly relevant for being up-to-date on referral sources). While these skills and knowledge can be acquired through lectures, workshops, courses and local support groups, they can also be acquired through reading journals and books. A mixture of both is probably desirable to achieve and maintain competence.

One of the major functions of supervision is to monitor the level of competence and functioning of the supervisee (see Section 1). It is a form of quality control for the profession. A supervisor would expect routinely to monitor the quantity of work a counsellor is undertaking. Overwork and stress can impair performance and thus competence.

A supervisor is also likely to pick up signs of mental illness and irrationality. They have a duty (BAC 1995: B.1.12) to draw the attention of a supervisee to this and help them decide how to deal with it. In the same clause of this code, the supervisor has the responsibility of assisting the counsellor in assessing whether 'personal or emotional difficulty' (BAC 1997: B.6.1.3) is impairing performance and judgement. This impaired performance might be because practice, cognitive function or ability to offer a secure containment are affected. In times of severe emotional distress, such as bereavement or separation from a partner, the counsellor might be tempted to turn to their client to meet their own emotional needs. Indeed some counselling organizations (e.g. CRUSE) would not select someone for training who has suffered a severe loss (bereavement, separation and divorce, major illness and so on) in the last two years. Some organizations also prohibit a counsellor from working for at least two weeks should they become bereaved. This is a good rule of thumb for any counsellor. After two weeks they would be advised to consult with their supervisor to decide whether they need a longer break from counselling.

All the BAC codes of ethics and practice make it clear that the counsellor, supervisor or trainer must not let their professional relationship be 'unduly influenced by their emotional needs'. Indeed, the supervisor's and trainer's codes both add that emotional needs must be met outside the supervisory or training work. Of course this is equally true for a counsellor and is the best way of ensuring that one does not turn to a client. As with other areas of potential incompetence the supervisor may also alert the counsellor if the client is being used inappropriately.

The central role of the supervisor in helping a counsellor assess their competence reinforces how important the supervisor is to a counsellor and also how critical the choice of that supervisor is. The counsellor must have a supervisor they can trust and from whom they will accept challenges about competence or fitness to practise. Simply relying on self-awareness and self-challenge would sometimes be inadequate. The centrality of the supervisor is highlighted in the code for counsellors (BAC 1997: B.6.3.1–B.6.3.3) where the details of the supervisory relationship are spelt out. Supervision is a formal, confidential relationship to ensure efficacy. It should happen regularly and frequently enough to reflect the level of experience of the counsellor and the volume of the work. Last but not least, where the line-manager and the counselling supervisor are the same person the counsellor must also receive supervision from a person who is independent of the counselling service.

Part of being a competent counsellor is providing an environment which is physically and emotionally stable and secure. If a counsellor has evidence of insecurity in the client he or she should be asking the cause of this and checking that it is not due to incompetence. At a practical level the counsellor needs to do a number of things related to safety to ensure the client's security. In particular, counsellors need to feel safe themselves (BAC 1997: B.6.2.1), which may mean ensuring someone is in the building when they are working and having a panic button or equivalent (Syme 1994). This precaution is of course to protect the client from the counsellor as well as vice versa. It cannot be assumed that only a client would become violent, although except in the case of self-defence this would be incompetence if not malpractice on the part of the counsellor.

Another way in which a safety net is ensured is by having professional indemnity insurance. UKCP stipulates that psychotherapists are 'required to ensure that their professional work is adequately covered by professional indemnity insurance' (UKCP 1998: 2.9), whereas BAC's Code for Counsellors requires its members to take it out and at an appropriate level of cover when needed (BAC 1997: B.6.1.6). It is possible that any counsellor could harm a client through making an error, through malpractice or by omissions, thus clients have a right of financial redress. For an employed counsellor or a volunteer counsellor in an agency, it is likely that professional indemnity insurance is put in place by the employer or the agency. It is essential that an independent practitioner buys their own (Syme 1994). This is a requirement of any independent counsellor who is registered by the United Kingdom Register of Counsellors (UKRC).

A client may be feeling unsafe because a counsellor has reached the limits of their competence. This will happen because counsellors are bound to be less experienced when they first start working. A counsellor may realize their lack of experience at the assessment or first session and refer the client to someone else immediately. It is also possible that it is later on in the relationship that a counsellor realizes a lack of experience, for instance in the specialist area of sexual abuse or severe mental illness. When this becomes apparent to the counsellor the client should be referred on to someone with the appropriate knowledge and skill (BAC 1997: B.6.1.4 and BPS 1998: 2.2 and 2.4). BPS not only directs the practitioner to work within the limits of their knowledge but also lays on the counselling psychologist the responsibility to ensure that anyone 'working under their direct supervision' (BPS 1998: 2.5) complies with the competence requirements of BPS.

There will be occasions when counsellors make mistakes, are aware that they have done so and are able to apologize and put it right. Counsellors can also feel or think they have made a mistake or are incompetent when this is not true. This frequently occurs when there is an ethical dilemma. Whenever this is so, it is essential to consult one's supervisor and/or other experienced practitioners (BAC 1997: B.6.1.7) to ascertain whether there is a basis for this feeling. Similarly, counsellors must do this when they are uncertain as to whether a particular situation or course of action may be in violation of a code.

BAC, BPS and UKCP all require that their members do not claim any false qualifications, nor advertise themselves incorrectly or allow others to do so, but only BPS lists this under competence (BPS 1998: 2.1 and 2.3). Clearly it is unethical and illegal to claim qualifications one does not possess.

A final way to check competence is to monitor and evaluate one's work. This can be done by routinely checking such things as how many clients do not take up the offer of counselling following assessment, how many clients stop suddenly and the average length of a counselling relationship. One could actually initiate research or take part in someone else's research using questionnaires to monitor client's satisfaction with the relationship established, the counsellor's work and the outcome of the work. All of these and other questions would help evaluate the quality and efficacy of a counsellor's work.

In summary it is essential that counsellors are open to their own and other's assessment of their competence and are prepared to take action as soon as they are aware of a problem.

Question 8

A counsellor wants to bring a counselling relationship to an end in the considered belief that the work is complete but the client disagrees – what issues should be considered in deciding a way forward?
Gabrielle Syme

The managing of endings is an essential skill for all therapists. Every session has an ending, as does the counselling relationship. Endings should be mentioned during the initial contracting. If the work is time-limited or short-term then this should be clear to the client and in every session the number of sessions left needs to be mentioned. In open-ended work there will be no set date for ending but it is good practice to build in regular reviews and give guidance on how endings happen.

In thinking about endings the practitioner needs to be aware of two issues specifically mentioned in the BAC *Code of Ethics and Practice for Counsellors* (1997). First, they should 'work with clients to reach a recognized ending when clients have received the help they sought or when it is apparent that counselling is no longer helping or when clients wish to end' (BAC 1997: B.1.3.8). Second, they must not 'exploit their clients financially or emotionally' (BAC 1997: B.1.3.2). A consequence of these two directives is that, apart from reviewing the work with the client, it is essential to discuss regularly in supervision the progress of the work and whether it is time for termination. Independent practitioners in particular are open to the charge of exploiting their client and maintaining their income by prolonging the counselling relationship. A counsellor should not have decided that the counselling work is complete without broaching this with the client and having a detailed discussion with a supervisor. For the counsellor and supervisor to reach this decision they will both have looked for evidence that the work was complete. The counsellor in particular will have observed clues to indicate this is so. Examples include the client being more aware of the counsellor's well-being or the client no longer being deeply distressed. Having found evidence, they are likely then to consider the impact on the client and the best ways to manage the ending. In this discussion they should have considered the presenting issues. If the client came because of a loss then this will impinge on the management of the ending. Another important consideration is how the client's early life story would affect the response to finishing the relationship – for example if the client had experienced traumatic losses such as bereavement, divorcing parents or emigration earlier in life. Linked with early losses is the possibility that the client has formed a highly dependent relationship. This could be exacerbated if the work has been long-term.

If a counsellor and a supervisor consider the work complete it would be poor practice for the counsellor to present this suddenly. Regardless of the life story of the client there should be a gradual testing of the readiness of the client to work towards an ending and, if ready, a plan made. This plan would take into account the life story of the client, the client's dependency needs, how the client has managed recent breaks for the counsellor's holidays, the level of fear about separation and the support available to the client in the outside world. In other words a lot of forethought and preparation must take place. Some counsellors actually create a rite of passage with their clients. Even if there is no created rite of passage, the end of therapy is a rite of passage in itself. Therefore it is very important that wherever possible the ending is planned, gradual and satisfies the client's emotional and developmental needs so that it is 'owned', feels significant and is freeing. It should be a good ending.

Not all endings will be good, despite careful planning. The most difficult are those where the client does not wish to end despite the counsellor's attempts to be sensitive with the timing and management of the ending. Of course a client may also not want to end because of insensitivity and mismanagement by the counsellor. So if a client disagrees about ending, the first step is to examine with oneself and one's supervisor such things as whether one has been clumsy, has missed some critical issue still to be resolved, has been insensitive to fear of separation or has not recognized the degree of dependency. If any of these are the case it is important for counsellors to acknowledge their misjudgement and continue working until the client is ready and 'wishes to end' (BAC 1997: B.1.3.8).

It is still possible for the counsellor, supported by his or her supervisor, to believe that the work is complete and for the client not to agree. There is then a conflict not only between the counsellor and client but also an internal struggle for the counsellor. On the one hand a 'counsellor's role is to facilitate the client's work in ways which respect the client's values, personal resources and capacity for choice' (BAC 1997: 3.1) and the counsellor 'must take care not to abuse their power' (BAC 1997: B.1.3.4). On the other hand, if counsellors really believe the work is complete they would not want to continue where there is a risk of being accused of exploiting the client financially (BAC 1997: B.1.3.2) and counsellors working ethically should not have to forfeit their fundamental right to professional honesty. This latter consideration does give counsellors the right to terminate the work despite clients' objections particularly where every care has been taken with their welfare.

If every effort has been made to end the work and still the client disagrees, the counsellor will have to accept that a good ending is not possible. Indeed this may be a necessary replica for the client of an earlier life experience. At this point a decision should be made and a date set and stuck to kindly and firmly without being punitive. It may be helpful to suggest to the client that if, after a period of reflection so that the therapeutic work can be internalized, there is still a conviction that counselling work is not complete, that would be the time to consider another counsellor. If the client was originally referred to the counsellor, then the referrer should be informed that counselling is ending. It is sensible also to ensure that one's supervisor is fully informed and thus is supportive, for one can feel very troubled, particularly if the client is very angry and attacking as the relationship ends. This may continue after the work has finished so here again supervision support is essential. At worst the former client could be so angry and hurt that a complaint is lodged. It is wise in such circumstances to protect oneself by making detailed notes of all the steps taken, particularly the use of supervision; this will indicate that due care and attention have been given to the client.

Question 9

How should I proceed when working with someone who expresses serious suicidal thoughts and feelings? What issues need considering?
Carol Shillito-Clarke

Suicide is a difficult issue for counsellors as it involves a complex interaction of ethics and legal responsibilities together with contextual, cultural and religious considerations. The decision-making processes are further complicated by the interaction between the strong personal feelings, beliefs and values of the therapist and those of the client. The core dilemma is how to balance respect for the client's right to decide whether to live or die against the counsellor's 'duty of care' to avoid misconceived and irreparable harm. The fidelity of the therapeutic relationship must also be set against the need to act in the client's best interest and possibly against the need to breach confidentiality in order to get more appropriate help.

Not everyone would agree with the proposition that a person has the right to take their own life. Some religions consider life to be sacred and suicide a sin. Since 1961, in England and Wales, it is no longer a crime to take one's own life but it is a criminal offence to assist someone else to do so. Many people who accept that suicide is neither a crime nor a sin would, nevertheless, consider that a person who is seriously contemplating killing themselves is not acting reasonably or rationally and is not of 'sound mind'. Such people would argue that anyone contemplating an act of self-harm should be dissuaded, and that they will be grateful for the intervention when they 'come to their senses'. The argument applies equally to all those threatening suicide, whether as a 'cry for help', as a result of experiencing psychiatric problems or as a serious alternative to facing personal circumstances. While the argument for counselling against suicide is persuasive, the counsellor needs to be fully aware of the beliefs and prejudices in themselves and in those around them – supervisor, employers, members of their culture and community – if they are to help the client to think through the dilemma.

Counsellors who work with a seriously suicidal client are forced to confront their own beliefs and prejudices. They must manage some very dark, powerful, sometimes destructive and often deep-seated emotions in themselves as well as those in their client. Existential fear of death; overwhelming feelings of anxiety, hopelessness, pain and anger; the sense of failure, the desire for control or revenge, all may be present consciously and unconsciously. At the same time, the counsellor is inevitably aware of the practical consequences of a client's suicide, which may include an inquest and formal inquiry procedures. They are likely to be faced with their own limitations as therapists: their ability to help another, to make a difference.

The counsellor working with a client who expresses serious suicidal ideation holds considerable power and responsibility. If one holds the ethical principles proposed by BAC, that a counsellor is 'responsible for working in ways which respect and promote the client's ability to make decisions in the light of his/her own beliefs, values and context' (BAC 1997: B.2.2), then it is not ethically acceptable to use the power imbalance in the counsellor–client relationship to impose one's own ideas and beliefs on the client or to try to coerce the client into a change of mind. Focusing on all the reason's why the client should live or suggesting that she or he is selfishly not considering the feelings of others are common mistakes.

Of course, counsellors have a right to their own feelings, beliefs and ideas. There may be occasions when a counsellor feels that they cannot give a suicidal client an unbiased hearing. In such cases the client needs to be helped to find someone who can. Any such bias needs to be declared at the initial contracting over limits of confidentiality rather than waiting until a relationship has been formed with the client. The disruption of even a tentative bond may further add to the client's negative perception of him or herself and their world. From the start, it is important that any expression of suicidal thought or idea is taken seriously. Thinking about suicide is not uncommon or pathological and talking about suicide does not increase the likelihood of the client taking action. Rather, it enables the client to express and feel heard for the desperation they are experiencing.

However, when suicide is being discussed it is often a struggle for the counsellor to contain their own and the client's anxieties sufficiently to allow the client to do their own work. The temptation may be to retreat from the individual's pain and hold to a theoretical construction of the client 'keeping them and what they arouse in us, at a safe distance' (Lemma 1996: 104). The counsellor may contain the anxiety by minimizing the extent of the client's desperation and suicidal intention, which can leave the client inadequately supported, uncontained and potentially at greater risk. Conversely, uncontained anxiety may lead to the counsellor prematurely arranging for medical intervention and hospitalization. If the client is not in full agreement with having their freedom curtailed in this way, then the fidelity of the therapeutic alliance may be seriously compromised. This may also have serious adverse consequences for future therapeutic help.

There is no fixed definition of 'duty of care' but counsellors, including trainees, must be able to demonstrate that they have taken the care and reasonable precautions that would be expected of a competent practitioner. The counsellor's first duty is to create a space in which the client can explore what suicide may mean to them while sensitively assessing the level of intent. The process of assessment for, and management of, suicidal intent is one for which every counsellor should have specific training in order to be able to meet the ethical requirements of competence. It may require that the counsellor interact with the client in a more directive way than their preferred style. Counsellors should ensure that they have debated the issues involved in taking active responsibility for the management of cases involving suicide before they attempt to do so. The appropriate use of supervision and access to good consultancy is vital, although counsellors need to be aware that others, including their supervisor, may not find the subject of suicide easy to deal with.

It is also important to remember that no counsellor is involved solely as a private individual. Even those in private practice have ethical responsibilities to colleagues, other professionals, funding bodies and the public perception of counselling (BAC 1997). If the counsellor is employed by an agency or institution which itself has relevant policies and procedures they must be taken into account. It is the counsellor's responsibility to be familiar with all such policies and procedures and to negotiate any significant difference between the employer's requirements and their own beliefs.

Suicide raises legal considerations. Committing suicide is not a crime but to aid, abet, counsel or procure the suicide of another constitutes a legal offence (Suicide Act 1961, Section 2 (1)). This has implications for the counsellor who has reason to believe that a client is about to commit suicide. While Bond (1999: 9) cites Menlowe and McCall Smith (1993) in stating that 'there is no general duty to rescue in British law', the law is complicated. In some settings there may be an obligation to break confidentiality and inform the medical services and police. To ignore that obligation may be challenged as professional negligence and a dereliction of the 'fiduciary' obligation to protect someone against themselves (Jenkins 1997; Bond 1999).

Wherever possible, the client's permission to break confidentiality, for example to their general practitioner, should be sought. The involvement of the GP does not automatically lead to full psychiatric in-patient care. It does enable the client to access other forms of support that may be important when the counsellor is not available. Sharing the weight of responsibility can also relieve pressure on the counsellor, enabling them to work more openly with the client. Dealing with a suicidal client is not a time for heroics or omnipotence.

Ultimately the responsibility for deciding whether or not to break confidentiality 'rests with the counsellor personally who must use professional judgement according to all the circumstances of the case. The counsellor must also be prepared to be personally accountable for the decision made' (Bond 1999: 3). In any circumstance, disclosing confidential information, particularly if the client withholds permission, needs to be 'restricted to relevant information, conveyed only to appropriate people and for appropriate reasons likely to alleviate the exceptional circumstances' (BAC 1997: B.3.4.2). Failure to observe such restrictions and guidelines could leavethe counsellor open to an ethical or legal complaint from the client.

Working with seriously suicidal clients can be intellectually and emotionally draining for the counsellor. It requires maintaining a delicate balance between, on the one hand, over-reacting and risking the fidelity of the therapeutic relationship and, on the other, denying the extent of the client's sense of meaninglessness and despair. It also requires competence in the process of assessing and managing the level of intention, acknowledgement of the importance of confidentiality in creating a safe space for exploration, and acceptance of responsibility for breaking that confidentiality in the client's best interest if necessary. Above all, it challenges the counsellor's deepest beliefs and feelings about the meaning of life and death and their relationship to others in their world.

Question 10

Does a counsellor have a responsibility to challenge a client's prejudices?
Roger Casemore

A dictionary definition of 'prejudice' states that it is 'a preconceived opinion or bias against or in favour of a person or thing' (Concise Oxford Dictionary, 1998), so my initial response to this question is that it depends on what the prejudice is as to if and how I will challenge it. In considering the question it is necessary to think how our prejudices are rooted in our internal, individual values and belief systems. As human beings we cannot exist without prejudices which may be either consciously or unconsciously held. We begin to form them from birth, developing likes and dislikes for all manner of things and people. These enable us to survive and to succeed in the environment in which we are born, grow, live and die. Our prejudices are rooted in our internal value systems and are demonstrated through our attitudes and behaviours, many of which we may not necessarily be aware of.

Our attitudes and behaviours are based on values, which are indicators pointing beyond themselves to a particular view of life. 'Introjected values' are imposed or handed down to us by our parents or society. 'Acquired or developed values' we develop for ourselves on the basis of our experiences of life and our relationships with other people. Both introjected and acquired values can be further divided into 'instrumental values', which are the beliefs we have about desirable ways of behaving and 'terminal values', which are the beliefs we have about the kind of person it is desirable to be. Instrumental values can be further divided into 'moral values' (if we violate these we feel guilty for doing wrong) and 'competence values' (if we violate these we feel ashamed of being inadequate). Values are further complicated by the fact that they can often be in conflict with each other. Two moral values such as 'behaving honestly' and 'behaving lovingly' can be in conflict with each other, as can two competence values such as 'behaving imaginatively' and 'behaving logically', and a moral value such as 'acting politely' can be in conflict with a competence value such as 'offering intellectual criticism'. Figure 5 may help to show that more simply.

All values can be said to have the characteristic of 'oughtness', they are beliefs which we consider that we ought to maintain. They are a set of standards that guide our activities, behaviours and relationships. They help us to create or resolve conflicts, to make decisions and choices and to express our needs. Our values lead us to take positions on social issues, religion and politics. They guide the way we present ourselves to other people and evaluate, judge, blame or praise ourselves or others. Values also define the relationships which we make and maintain and are used as standards to persuade and influence other people and to tell ourselves which beliefs, attitudes, actions and values of other people are worth accepting. Values are a distinctly human characteristic not shared by other species. They allow us to maintain and enhance our self-esteem, no matter

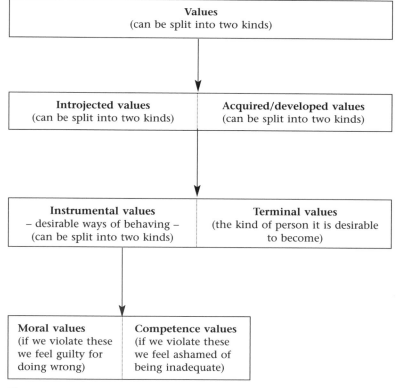

Figure 5 The structure of values

how socially undesirable our motives, feelings or actions may be. They are also clearly an integral part of and indivisible from our prejudices.

As a therapist, I regularly find myself working with clients whose introjected value systems create huge problems for them in living their daily lives. As children they received introjected values which caused them to believe that they must be a certain way and behave in certain ways in order to achieve the strongly conditional love of their parents or whoever was involved in bringing them up. These 'conditions of worth' (Rogers 1959) are carried through into adult life with the belief that these same ways of being and behaving are essential to achieving the love and acceptance of the self and of others. Part of my function as a therapist is to enable clients to identify where introjected values and conditions of worth are preventing them from living in satisfying and resourceful ways and to enable them to recognize that they can choose to change or modify their values and beliefs about themselves. A key part of my role is to enable clients to experience full acceptance from me, in order to work towards reversing those internalized, negative conditions of worth, by becoming more accepting of themselves and developing a more centralized locus of evaluation of the self, within themselves.

All therapists, no matter what their modality, seek to offer acceptance and unconditional positive regard to their clients. Unconditional positive regard does not mean accepting everything a client does or says or thinks as being right, neither does it mean accepting or condoning behaviours and activities which are clearly anti-social or illegal. The BAC code (1997: B.1.1) states, 'The counsellor–client relationship is the foremost ethical concern. However, counselling does not exist in social isolation. Counsellors may need to consider other sources of ethical responsibility.'

Counsellors must at all times consider their responsibility to others outside the counselling relationship, particularly where a client may be in danger of causing harm to others by their actions and behaviour. Some attitudes and values can be evidenced as more extreme forms of prejudice, such as those against other people who are different in some way, and when evidence of the existence of these in a client arises in therapy, ethically they cannot be ignored.

I believe that I have an ethical responsibility to challenge my client's prejudices and that different prejudices need to be challenged in different ways. My client may demonstrate prejudices that indicate extreme negative feelings towards other individuals or social groups in a way that gives rise to feelings of concern in me that they might act out those attitudes against the people or groups concerned. I believe it is right to disclose those feelings of mine in an appropriate way, within the counselling relationship. I need to do this in such a way that it is clear that I am not being judgemental about my client as a person, but that I do not hold the same views as them. If my client is actually describing anti-social or illegal behaviour of an extreme prejudicial nature against individuals or social groups because of their difference, then clearly I need to challenge that, confirming that I do not accept or condone such behaviours and probably stating that I cannot keep such revelations confidential. If I knowingly keep secret disclosures of serious harmful activity towards others, I am clearly in breach of the ethical principles of counselling (BAC 1997: B.1.6.1) and I might also be committing a criminal act, in making myself an accessory to those activities. Jenkins (1997) describes how a therapist

- is *required* to pass on information on terrorist offences,
- *may* be required to report suspected child abuse, depending on their employment contract, and
- *may* break confidentiality to report serious crime, including drug trafficking offences.

In the case of disclosures of serious crime, Bond (1993) states that the law is much more clear about not maintaining confidentiality and quotes the legal maxim 'there is no confidence in iniquity'. Disclosures might need to be made to a client's GP or a psychiatrist, to a social worker or even to a police officer. Jenkins (1997) recommends that the therapist considering such action should take expert legal advice from their professional indemnity insurer or their professional association before breaching confidentiality.

Not all prejudices are extreme or socially harmful, some are useful and important for our survival. Some prejudices, while not serious, may well affect or limit the way that clients live their lives. It can be most helpful for the therapist to challenge the client in a gentler way, by drawing the therapist's experiencing of prejudices in the client to the client's attention, in order to enable the client to choose to explore these prejudices. A constant element in my work with clients seems to be about enabling them to understand that they have a choice about how they view their world and themselves within it and that they can choose to challenge their introjected conditions of worth and change their attitudes and prejudices in order to live a more resourceful and satisfying life.

The nature of my challenge to prejudice depends in part on the nature of my relationship with the client and to some extent on the nature of the individual as well. Perhaps even more important than challenging prejudice in my clients is the need to identify and challenge prejudice within myself. The code (BAC 1997: A.2) states that 'counsellors must consider and address their own prejudices and stereotyping and ensure that an anti-discriminatory approach is integral to their counselling practice'.

For me, my holding discriminatory negative prejudices against individuals or social groupings that are in some way different from me is in itself unethical. It is important to be ethical in my approach to life and not just in my work with clients. It is quite invidious to think that I can switch my ethical principles on and off depending on whether I am counselling or not. It is essential to develop a real awareness of my values, attitudes and prejudices and of my own introjected conditions of worth so that they do not prevent me from living a satisfying and resourceful life, and that they do not limit the effectiveness of my relationships with my clients. If one of the ethical principles of counselling is the importance of valuing difference in our clients no matter what that difference may be, I must work hard to ensure that I am able to do that without the undue influence of inappropriate prejudices and ignorance. I also need to make sure that my natural prejudice against people who have strong prejudices which are different to mine does not prevent me from valuing or prizing them as individuals within the counselling relationship. I must not allow my prejudices or those of my client to unduly influence my relationship with the client and prevent me from working with them. A client may choose to maintain prejudices which I find totally unacceptable and this could lead me to the conclusion that I am unable to sustain a working relationship with them. In that case I can choose to make an effective and ethical referral, or arrive at an ethical ending. This is probably the strongest challenge of any that I could make to a client.

Question 11

The client fails to come to the next session – do you contact the client? How might the setting of the counselling also influence the decision?
Gabrielle Syme

There is no guidance in the ethical codes available to counsellors about whether or not to contact a client who has missed a pre-planned session without forewarning the counsellor. Central to the counsellor's decision should be respect for the client's autonomy, including the right to miss a session (BAC 1997: B.2.2).

The handling of missed and cancelled sessions should be made clear in the initial contracting (BAC 1997: B.4.3.1). This is particularly important in independent practice, where the client must know whether or not they have to pay for a missed appointment. In addition, if clients have to pay, it must be clear whether all missed sessions are charged for or whether there are extenuating circumstances in which this rule would not be applied. It is equally important for a client of a counselling agency or a client funded by an employer or EAP, particularly when the contract is time-limited, to know whether the missed session is counted as a session and therefore forfeited when missed, and whether there are rules such as the missing of a session being understood as the termination of the contract, or counselling automatically terminating after a specified number of sessions have been missed. If the clients know the consequences of missing a session then when one is missed it is clearly their choice, whether conscious or unconscious.

When the contract is explicit, and particularly with long-term work, it is often unnecessary for a counsellor to contact the client over one missed session. One must then decide how to work out the significance of the missed session in subsequent sessions, how many sessions are missed before making contact and how to make contact.

The reasons for a missed session could be simple, such as a sudden crisis leaving no time to inform the therapist. If this is the case, clients usually ring as soon as they can to explain their absence. More often the significance of a missed session can be complicated. Clients may insist that they 'just forgot'. For many counsellors, particularly psychodynamic ones, 'forgetting' is an unconscious and significant act. It could be evidence of inner chaos and turmoil, an attack on the therapy and therapist or ambivalence about receiving counselling at all. If the absence occurs immediately after a break in therapy caused by the therapist it could be a punishment of the therapist – a 'tit-for-tat' for 'making' the client miss a session. Another dynamic acted out through a missed session consists of testing whether the therapist really accepts and is committed to a client's autonomy or will be punitive over a lack of notification of absence. In a sense, the client is being rebellious. At other times, absence may indicate the client's need to be mischievous.

Sometimes the counsellor will have a very strong premonition that the session is going to be missed. It may be that the client's need to act out something is being unconsciously communicated. It is also not uncommon to have some strong feelings during the missed session. It is important, therefore, that counsellors take note of what they think and feel before and during a missed session. This should be explored in supervision when thinking about working out the meaning of the absence in subsequent sessions. Anger may indicate an attack on the therapy or a challenge by the rebellious client. Fear may also indicate an attack. Anxiety may be a concern about the client's welfare but it may also be a counter-transference response related to the client's need to be special.

Exploration to discover the significance of a missed session should be done in the spirit of enquiry rather than accusingly. It is sometimes much later in the therapy that a client makes sense of a missed session.

There is no hard and fast rule about how many sessions should be missed before making contact. It is important to discuss this with one's supervisor and to take into account such things as the life story of the client, the possible significance of the break, the reasons for entering therapy, the stage one has reached in the therapy, recent breaks in the therapy caused by the counsellor, the current life events for the client and the possible fear of punishment.

At some point contact should be made and in such a way that the client's right to autonomy is balanced against genuine concern about the client's welfare and the possible significance in the therapy of the missed session. This is a complicated balancing act and is probably best done in a letter. This is also less intrusive and less demanding for the client. The letter should give clients permission not to come or even permission to end if this is their desire but also suggest that meeting would be a better way to make sense of what is happening.

In general, if the contract on missed sessions is clear, it is unnecessary to contact a client after one missed session. However, there are specific occasions and contexts where it is necessary or desirable to make contact. One example is if the missed session is the initial session: it may be the result of a change of mind, fear, anxiety or ambivalence. A brief letter may be helpful so that the client is encouraged to come or freed from the obligation. Another example is when a client misses the last session, perhaps because the ending is unbearable. This will leave the counsellor feeling the work is incomplete. This can be dealt with in supervision but a 'goodbye' letter to the client may be useful to both parties so that the work is complete.

A context in which it would be important to write after a missed session is in the case of an agency offering free counselling at the point of delivery to people with chaotic lives, possibly caused by homelessness or addiction problems. It is often difficult for them to keep appointments and they often have low self-esteem and do not believe they are important to anyone. A letter would indicate that they are remembered and that there will be no recrimination and would also remind them of the time of the next appointment. The letter in itself could be immensely therapeutic.

Some counsellors and clients do not plan sessions in advance. There are many reasons for this. Some therapies, for instance solution-focused therapy, make no assumptions about how many sessions are needed, but decide at each session whether there is to be another one. Some clients are too fearful to arrange more than one session at a time. Sometimes the client or therapist has been uncertain about an appointment time for a few weeks later and may have agreed to arrange that at the next session; if this session is missed then this cannot be done. In all these instances it will be necessary to make contact. In this situation a telephone call would be appropriate, but it must always be remembered that telephone calls are intrusive and demanding and confidentiality may require that a message cannot be left on an answerphone or with whoever answers the call. If in any doubt a letter is better, not least because the counsellor can plan what is written and take the necessary care over the content. As in all counselling work, forethought to ensure the client's safety and well-being is essential.

Question 12

A couple enter counselling and it quickly becomes apparent that the female partner is very largely dependent on the man. Evidence quickly accumulates indicating that the dependence is being used by the man to coerce the woman to adopt patterns of eating and of physical and sexual behaviour that have reduced her to a very debilitated state. Yet she adores him and has no complaint. It is he who complains that she is untrustworthy. He shows no awareness of the harm being done to his partner, nor of his coercive behaviour. What ethical issues require consideration?
Derek Hill

The situation summarized is illustrative of the complexity of the ethical issues which face couple counsellors. As the first of the couple-work scenarios here it will be given an expanded treatment which will set out issues that are common to many of the dilemmas faced in this form of counselling.

Good practice demands that every aspect of such a situation is given separate consideration. Only then is it possible to assess the ways in which each ethical issue interacts with the others, and thus how any action taken to address the perceived dilemma may impact on the couple, the individual partners, and on their relationship with the counsellor.

1 'A couple enter counselling'

This phrase raises two questions:

- What is the basis of the relationship between 'the couple' and the counsellor?
- Who or what is the counsellor's client?

Clause 3.2 of the BAC *Code of Ethics and Practice for Counsellors* (1997) offers a description of a working relationship based on 'a deliberately undertaken contract' between counsellor and clients, and the implication is that such a contract must itself conform to the content of the code if the transaction is properly to be described as counselling. What is less clear from the code is who, or what, is the 'client'. Each partner might reasonably say, 'I am your client' or 'he/she has the problem and is the client'. The counsellor might say, 'as a couple counsellor I have contracted with this couple to address their relationship as the client'. None of those assertions is necessarily a sound basis on which to build a contract for counselling.

The reality is that, in common with other forms of counselling, couple counselling is undertaken on the basis of working relationships which are the outcome of, and subject to, both explicit negotiation and more subtle, implicit or even unconscious transformations. Couple counselling can be seen as a complex sequence of manoeuvres in which the partners seek to modify the nature of their relationships with each other and with the counsellor, forming and breaking alliances as the priorities which they give to personal safety, or the well-being of the couple relationship, change. If the counsellor monitors these shifts and interprets them in terms of a focus on a 'client' designated and agreed with the partners, those manoeuvres become a rich source of insights into the nature of the couple relationship.

If there is a lack of clarity about the identity of the client, or if that focus for the work is allowed to change without explicit negotiation, the consequences are profound. First, the counselling contract is invalid or has been breached, which renders the working relationship unethical. Second, the uncertain identity of the client creates a situation in which no stable therapeutic alliance can be established, containment is impossible, and the significance of transactions between the counsellor and the partners is obscured. Those transactions may subsequently prove harmful to the couple relationship, and to the partners individually.

We might hypothesize that, at the moment when the counsellor in our scenario asked 'and what should I do about this situation?', the prime focus of concern was the woman's well-being (client–victim), the context was the coercive/persecutory relationship, and the man was perceived to be the oppressor (the Other). In this case the influence of the counsellor's value system has resulted in the abandonment of a focus on the couple relationship as client, and has established in the counsellor's mind the need for a contract based on the victim–persecutor–rescuer dynamic of the 'drama triangle'. At that time it is likely that the woman's contract was to work on preserving the all-important relationship (client) with her partner. His contract might be 'focus on turning her (client) into the trustworthy person I deserve'.

For the reasons explained, this hypothetical situation calls for the counsellor's urgent action if an ethical basis is to be found for the work which is to follow.

2 'The female partner is very largely dependent on the man'

This statement, alone, may not raise an ethical issue for the counsellor. On the other hand, a counsellor attuned to feminist thinking may well see the couple relationship to be an expression of the man's conscious or unconscious male chauvinism. If so, the ethical issue faced has to do with the appropriateness of a direct challenge to the man's value system. The basic values identified in the code are *integrity*, *impartiality* and *respect* (BAC 1997: A) and it may be that the counsellor's dilemma centres on the need to sustain a personal integrity by voicing that challenge rather than appearing to collude with the man, even for a few moments.

We can hypothesize that the counsellor's immediate response to this issue is to delay any challenge and to set about gathering the evidence which will either affirm a gender-based power differential or uncover other, or additional, attributes in the partners which have resulted in their particular 'marital fit' (Dicks 1967). This hypothesis allows us space to consider other issues in the casework. It envisages the counsellor being alert to gendered behaviours and to the ways in which the partners' differing processes of socialization may have predisposed them to seek and sustain a form of relationship in which neither has the space to realize potential or fulfil fundamental aspirations.

3 'It is he who complains that she is untrustworthy'

The male client presents the counsellor with his rationale for seeking help – his partner is untrustworthy. Here we have a bid to make the woman the client and the immediate issue is whether the counsellor is faced with partners whose agendas are different or shared.

If the agendas are different, the counsellor is being asked to engage in the complexities of work that can have no predetermined outcome. He or she must be committed to supporting both partners as they explore their own and each other's perceptions, needs and aspirations, with the possibility that either or both partners may conclude that their differences are irreconcilable, or that jointly they can find an accommodation. If this work and the associated contract is adopted, the counsellor's issue is one of 'even-handedness' or, in the words of the code, *impartiality* (BAC 1997: A). These situations test the couple counsellor to the limit. There may well be three different value systems active in the counselling room. There will certainly be a gender imbalance in the three people engaged in the work. The issues raised may evoke the most primitive of emotions in both the partners and the counsellor. The counsellor will be called on to be sufficiently self-aware to be able to recognize and discount the need to resolve personal conflicts so as to hear and relate to the partners' individual and shared issues. The skills will be needed with which to create a 'safe place' in which the partners may each test their own realities and address each other's. The desire to act impartially may exist. But the counsellor must make a careful judgement about whether the work in prospect can be underpinned with the necessary competence and, if not, should refer the couple to a more skilled practitioner.

If the partners agree about the causes of the conflict between them and show a willingness to collaborate in efforts to resolve matters there is likely to be little difficulty in agreeing an agenda which puts their relationship in the client role. This form of shared agenda may present few ethical issues and can yield substantial benefits for the couple. However, the counsellor may quickly become aware that the material which the couple are offering is relatively superficial and that the roots of their conflict lie in more fundamental issues. Therapeutically, it may be judged that failure to address those underlying issues will leave the couple vulnerable to further conflict and ill-equipped to resolve it. Assessments of this kind commonly lead to work involving a number of renegotiations of the counselling contract and a progressive deepening of the work. That form of case management is grounded in a commitment to *respect* the partners perceptions and to avoid any abuse of the power differential that exists between them and the counsellor (BAC 1997: B.1.3.4). Those who offer brief therapy, and all who work with clients exposed to internal or external risk which is serious or increases as time passes, may not have the option of planning on the basis of progressively developed contracts. In such circumstances the initial assessment must devote special attention to the couple's individual and shared resources and their capacities to tolerate and make creative use of a more dynamic form of counselling. The ethical judgement required is not to do with how much confrontation and coercion the partners can withstand without causing lasting harm, but how flexible and responsive they are with one another, and how creatively they use the counsellor's interventions. It follows that time-bounded work and that which addresses serious risk puts a premium on assessment and casework skills, as well as on the capacity to weigh ethical issues.

4 'The dependence is being used by the man to coerce the woman to adopt patterns of eating and of physical and sexual behaviour that have reduced her to a very debilitated state . . . He shows no awareness of the harm being done to his partner, nor of his coercive behaviour'

Harm is being done to the woman. The man appears unaware of the nature of his behaviour or the serious impact it has on his partner's well-being. There is the risk of further harm to the woman and there is a need to do something. Should I notify the local domestic violence unit, make a referral for a psychiatric assessment or suspend further work with the couple until he has had personal therapy?

The female partner is described as 'very debilitated', although no specific forms of harm are mentioned, nor is there specific evidence that the debilitation is progressive or directly linked with patterns of behaviour which the male partner may be influencing. The male partner is reported not to see a connection between his wife's condition and any negative influence he may have on her. He is also said to believe that the influence he exerts on her is of an acceptable form. The situation *may* require action which offers the female partner protection, and which addresses the husband's behaviour; it certainly requires further investigation.

These alternative responses might come from the counsellor and the counsellor's supervisor. They might also be two perspectives which the counsellor can voice. Casement (1985) refers to an 'internal supervisor' and the capacity to adopt a 'meta-position' relative to the case material. That is something which many experienced counsellors can do when not too tired, too stressed by casework or too filled with specific anxieties prompted by personal issues raised in a particular case. This is not the place to explore how that internal supervisor can be installed and sustained, but it must be clear that when faced with ethical issues it is an invaluable internal resource in striving to hold a balance between the disciplines of counselling and the powerful influences of a personal value system, intuition, personal resonances, and a perhaps omnipotent sense of a duty of care.

That internal supervisor can assist in the conduct of essential processes which may be summarized as follows:

- standing back,
- questioning the sense that there is no time to reflect,
- listening to and understanding the roots of (conflicting) emotional responses,
- questioning whether the evidence actually supports the initial assessment of the situation,
- putting it on paper,
- if necessary, gathering more information from the clients,
- when there is enough material to talk about, testing it all out with your supervisor or a trusted senior colleague,
- listening to your supervisor,
- identifying *all* the options available as responses to these aspects of the partners' situations and
- delaying any decision about a preferred option for action until all aspects of the case have been considered and it is possible to determine the action which offers the best balance between the ethical principles of beneficence and non-maleficence (see Section 1).

5 'Yet she adores him and has no complaint'

Although apparently at risk, she does not see this as an issue and wants their couple relationship to continue. It is possible that her involvement in the counselling is itself the result of the male partner's coercion as well as her own wish to be seen by him as trustworthy. It is not unusual to find an individual engaging in couple counselling because of the partner's coercion as well as a desire for their own needs to be met. However, this woman appears to be the subject of an abusive relationship and may not be able to protect herself from further harm.

Couple counsellors are continually confronted by intimate relationships which they themselves could not tolerate for a moment, but which the partners freely choose to sustain. *Respect* and avoidance of *advice-giving* or of *acting on behalf of clients* in all but exceptional circumstances (BAC 1997: A, B.1.3.6, B.1.3.5) define ethical practice in that situation. But clause B.3.4.1 recognizes that a client may be at risk of *suffering serious harm* and may be *no longer willing or able to take responsibility for his/her own actions*. In such a case it may be ethical to *breach confidentiality* (normally after discussion with the client) in order to fulfil the duty of care. Thus the counsellor must consider

- whether the woman has suffered, or is at risk of, serious harm,
- whether she appears to retain a capacity to protect her own well-being,
- if apparently unable to protect herself, whether that assessment can be confirmed by a person professionally equipped for that task, and
- if 'incompetent', what steps should be taken to offer her protection.

Responding to the dilemma

We do not at this stage have sufficient information to reach a decision about what action the counsellor should take.

We have seen that there is uncertainty about the identity of the 'client' and the nature of the counselling contract. Whatever happens, those issues need clarification through negotiation (1).

The man's attitudes and values may place the counsellor in a situation in which he or she feels obliged for integrity's sake to address them directly and without delay (2).

The couple may be wishing to address a split or a shared agenda. This may necessitate a further renegotiation of the contract (3).

The husband does not recognize the nature or consequences of his behaviour towards his wife. There may be cause to report the situation to a domestic violence unit, or he may require psychiatric assessment, personal therapy or a psycho-educational intervention (4).

The wife appears to be wanting to be seen as trustworthy and to remove the discord in the relationship. She appears unconcerned about her physical and emotional state and may be incompetent to protect herself. She may need a medical or psychiatric assessment and subsequent protective action on her behalf (5).

More information about the partners and their relationship, the advice of medical or psychiatric practitioners, a re-examination of the counsellor's own agenda, and further negotiation with the couple and/or the individual partners could result in action ranging from

- an extended series of sessions with a focus on the couple's relationship

to

- referral of the woman to a refuge and disclosure of the man's behaviour towards her to a domestic violence unit.

These extremes, and every kind of intervention in between, should result from striking a balance between the five broad areas of ethical concern that have been identified. Whatever the decision, the couple counsellor will be acutely aware that a potentially dramatic and life-changing intervention has been made in at least two lives. Commonly the repercussions of such decisions affect children, grandparents and other family members as well. Lacking the gift of always making the 'right' decision, those who work with couples and their families carry a very clear responsibility to ensure that their actions are soundly grounded in the realities of their clients' lives and in a professional consensus about what ethical practice requires.

Question 13

Neil is confined to a wheelchair and has an untreatable degenerative condition. He and partner Doug seek couple counselling and make it apparent that they want to set up a contract between them which would lead Doug to give Neil a lethal dose of drugs when Neil appears no longer able to tolerate his own deterioration. The counsellor is asked to monitor negotiation between the partners to ensure that no hidden agendas distort the contract both say they want. What ethical issues require consideration?
Derek Hill

The term 'medically assisted suicide' was adopted in the context of a revision of guidelines issued in 1995 by the Royal Dutch Medical Association on 'active' or 'positive' euthanasia. The Netherlands has a history of liberal policy in this area. Australia's Northern Territory adopted legislation in 1996 making that form of medical intervention legal. While there have been pro-euthanasia movements in the United Kingdom since 1935, and in the USA since 1938, attitudes to euthanasia remain strongly influenced by the major religions' condemnation of the act in its active, passive and voluntary forms. Those acts are performed secretly throughout the world so there are no reliable statistics by which to gauge the scale of the practices. 'Living wills', which require an individual's medical carers not to make use of life support systems if the person becomes terminally ill or permanently unconscious or is irrevocably brain damaged, are being used increasingly to set limits on medical interventions. World-wide, opinion remains divided about the morality and ethics of the various forms of euthanasia. It is an issue about which counsellors might be expected to develop an informed opinion and which it is recognized may lead them to refuse to be party to the making of arrangements for euthanasia in any of its forms.

If Neil and Doug's counsellor is willing to work with the couple to explore the issues raised by the setting up of a contract for active euthanasia, the context in which that work will take place must be considered. If the counselling will be undertaken as part of an institutionally based service it is essential that, while not identifying the clients, the counsellor takes advice from an employment lawyer about the (probable) obligation to seek the employer's permission to undertake work with that specific focus. Organizations differ in their stances on such issues. Some bar such work and regard its unauthorized conduct as a disciplinary matter. Others may view the issue as something that should be determined by reference to the professional body. Others see such work as an enactment of liberal policies which they publicly support. If the matter is formally brought to the attention of an organization it would be prudent for that body to take legal advice about its own liabilities and those of its employees in a situation in which the nature of the counselling, the existence of the contract between the partners, or the act of euthanasia, became the subject of litigation. The stance of the organization on social policies may or may not override concerns about potential liabilities. No advice is offered here because of the contentious nature of the subject area.

It will be evident that institutionally based counsellors may not be free to act in accord with their consciences without risk to their employment and reputation.

If the counsellor is a self-employed person, taking the advice of the professional body is an essential step in deciding whether or not to work with Neil and Doug. Organizations such as the British Association for Counselling often take legal advice before giving an individual member guidance on such an issue. However, it is a matter of conscience whether the practitioner adheres to the guidance given. To act contrary to guidance raises the issue of continuing membership of the professional body. Acting against given advice normally results in the body withdrawing support from the individual if litigation takes place. If the counsellor plans to act contrary to the professional body's guidance, he or she would be prudent to establish whether their professional indemnity insurance cover will remain operative. If not, the ethics of counselling without appropriate insurance cover must be considered (BAC 1997: B.6.1.6). Prudence also requires that the counsellor takes direct legal advice before making a commitment to the counselling. Lastly, the counsellor may experience difficulties in identifying someone who is equipped and prepared to supervise the proposed casework. Failure to engage in regular supervision or, by implication, the exclusion of particular casework from supervision is unethical (BAC 1997: B.6.3.3).

If all the issues discussed here have been dealt with and the counsellor is able to engage with Neil and Doug, the ethical issues raised by the counselling contract will require similar careful attention. Confidentiality is an immediate concern, particularly as it relates to records, supervision and sources of expert advice. A review of the broad context in which the work will take place may raise issues that must be addressed by the contract. The partners' assurance that the content and process of the counselling will always be private is an important part of this kind of contract because it affirms the very precise purposes and limits of the work. Criteria and arrangements are needed to enable either the counsellor or one of the partners to end the joint work. A preliminary agreement is required about the nature and purposes of further contact with the clients after the end of the first cycle of counselling. The couple speak of shared purposes and of the possibility that either one of them may have 'agendas' of which they are unaware. From the couple counsellor's viewpoint the question is whether the partners have a shared or a split agenda, the former being the basis on which the couple wish to contract with each other. Given the uncertainty, it is essential that the counselling contract makes explicit the possibility that the partners may not achieve the contract for active euthanasia which they seek.

A 'no contract' outcome is not inevitable if, as is likely, the partners are subject to differing motivating factors. The issue is whether or not the influences operating on each of them are understood and acceptable to the other. The scope and the limits of the counselling are defined by this question. The partners are seeking insights into the psychological processes involved in establishing, living with and ultimately enacting a contract for active euthanasia. This will involve a very thorough exploration of their individual beliefs and values, and of their inner worlds. It will test their mutual trust as the dynamics of their relationship are explored and perhaps modified. It will reveal how each makes decisions, and how they make them jointly. The culmination of the work will be the individual and joint informed decisions about whether they can trust themselves as a couple, and each other as individuals, to extend their relationship by making a commitment to active euthanasia. Thereafter, the partners' task will be to build into the detail of their contract the checks and balances which take account of the psychological factors they have learned about. They will also need to incorporate information from various experts, and make arrangements which respond to the external influences they are likely to experience as they live with and enact it. If the partners engage in this detailed planning they may, or may not, wish to do it in the presence of the counsellor. If they choose to continue working with the counsellor the ethical challenge will lie in the temptation to 'know best' and to intervene in areas outside competence.

The ethical quality of the counselling provided for Neil and Doug depends on judgements made about whether it enabled them to exercise their autonomy individually and as a couple by making a complex set of informed decisions about their future (BAC 1997: B.2.2). Such judgements can never be conclusive because those concerned can never claim to know every influence at work during the counselling. In common with most other ethical enquiries, the best outcome that can be hoped for is a statement that there is no evidence of unethical behaviour. This fact draws attention to one of the realities of the counsellor's role: it is never possible to be certain that casework is unflawed. When that casework deals with life-and-death matters, as in the case of Neil and Doug, the consequence is that the counsellor may carry burdensome doubts long after contact with the clients has ended. Dedicated efforts to understand and address the many influences which can result in unethical practice are not only a source of protection for clients, they also offer the counsellor the assurance that every reasonable step was taken to avoid bad practice.

Question 14

What are a counsellor's responsibilities when an adult client discloses childhood sexual abuse and where the perpetrator(s) may still be abusing?
Caroline Jones

This question presents a testing moral and ethical dilemma for counsellors whose responsibilities depend on a number of factors. These include

- the purpose of this counselling relationship as determined by the client,
- the setting of the counselling,
- the awareness by the client of the safety of others as a possible consideration,
- the wishes of the client,
- the degree of risk and, finally,
- the counsellor's responsibilities under any codes or guidelines.

The purpose of this counselling relationship is central to this question. Disclosure of childhood sexual abuse within a confidential relationship and the wish for healing could be the client's only purpose for seeking counselling. Alternatively these events might have been disclosed purely as background to other or current difficulties that the client wishes to explore. Understanding and accepting the client's aims and goals in counselling must be the priority for the counsellor and these will determine the pace at which some of the other factors outlined above may arise during the counselling.

The setting of the counselling can be an important factor in determining the counsellor's responsibility. There is no duty in law to take any action. Nor does the Children Act 1989 place an automatic duty on counsellors to pass on information concerning children at risk. An exception occurs when the counselling is provided by an agency with a contractual obligation to pass on such information. Friel (1998) states that this obligation could be subject to 'challenge both in judicial review and indeed private law claims'. A counsellor working in such a setting makes clear the limits to confidentiality to clients during contracting and in pre-counselling literature.

The awareness of the client of the safety of others as a possible consideration is an important factor to consider and exploration of this might be on the client's agenda at some point during the counselling. Some clients may have already taken all reasonable steps to protect vulnerable children; this is more likely when the clients are clear that they were abused and that they were victims. Other clients might be struggling with the thought that their memories are confused, inaccurate or false. Sometimes the counsellor is sure that the abuse has occurred (evidence of indicators that point to childhood abuse plus the sense that the memories are real) while the client may still be at a stage of seeking certainty that the memories are real. In these circumstances the counsellor must exercise particular caution (McGuire 1997). Another possibility occurs when clients feel somehow responsible for the abusive events, so it follows that they may not consider that any other child could be at risk. These views may change after further exploration of the abusive events. Sometimes clients disclose within the counselling relationship as a first step to making a more public disclosure to other family members or to the police or other authorities. In these circumstances, this element in the purpose of the counselling is clear and the counsellor has no other responsibility than to work with the client's agenda and timetable.

The wishes of the client are the priority throughout the counselling. For some clients the thought of reporting the perpetrator(s) may seem too painful. The counsellor can consider offering accurate information about the channels of reporting and the possible consequences if, in their judgement, this will not unduly influence the client. The counsellor must, at the same time, demonstrate impartiality about the client's decisions. Sensitivity is also essential in order not to introduce or reinforce feelings of shame or blame by focusing on the issue of protecting other children who might be at risk with clients who are already feeling vulnerable. Client autonomy is enhanced when the counsellor encourages the client to undertake research outside the counselling room in order that any decisions are based on current and accurate information. One resource is the Accuracy About Abuse website. Another is to suggest that clients seek legal advice (BASRT 1996, reviewed 1999: 1.9). Disclosure may lead to a number of distressing consequences: little action by the authorities, failure to prosecute or gain convictions, disbelief, family splits and denial; all have the potential for leaving the client feeling more damaged. On the other hand, disclosure to the authorities by the client may be an empowering step towards healing.

Both the counsellor and the client might wish to explore the current *degree of risk*. If, on examination, the perpetrators seem no longer to have opportunities to abuse, this might be a factor in any decision about reporting the past crimes.

Counsellors will want to reread any *codes and guidelines* to ensure that they are aware of their professional responsibilities. A member of BAC reflects upon the clauses in the code concerning responsibilities to those at risk of serious harm (BAC 1997: B.3.4.1) and faces an ethical dilemma. The conflicting ethical priorities of the confidentiality and duty of care owed to the client, respecting client autonomy, doing most good and causing least harm within this counselling relationship and the public interest in protecting children at risk all need balancing one against another. Bringing the issue to counselling supervision would be a priority. Discussion within counselling supervision allows time for exploration of all aspects of the case and the significance, if any, of the timing of the counselling relationship as well as the content. Additionally, this issue can arouse strong feelings in both counsellor and client and the counsellor needs support within counselling supervision to contain their own feelings in order best to help the client. Finally, a counsellor who does decide to break confidentiality 'must also be prepared to be personally accountable for the decisions made, if they are challenged by a complaint to a professional organization or in the courts' (Bond 1999: 3).

Counsellors are aware that one consequence of disclosure of abuse is that this can lead to the accusations that the memories are false and that the counsellor is incompetent or worse. The counselling profession and individual counsellors can deal with these consequences by pointing to research (McGuire 1997). There are no easy answers to the dilemmas raised by this issue. What is more certain is that by listening and staying with the pain of the memories, the counsellor can help the client.

Question 15

At assessment, a potential client tells me she has been seeing another counsellor for some time but wants to make a change – the other counsellor is unaware of this so how should I proceed?
Gabrielle Syme

Counsellors should always try to establish at assessment whether a potential client is involved in any other therapeutic relationship. Of course this is not possible if the client chooses not to reveal any other therapeutic relationship. If it is established that another therapeutic relationship exists the counsellor has 'to consider whether counselling is appropriate' (BAC 1997: B.1.3.7).

If the therapeutic relationship is with a psychiatrist or psychologist and involves regular check-ups but no therapy it may well be appropriate to offer counselling as well. Assessment will ascertain this. However, counselling should only be offered with the knowledge and agreement of the other mental health professional(s). Agreement can be obtained by letter or telephone call, provided the potential client has agreed to this contact. If they have not and it is only hearsay that there is agreement it would be unwise to offer a counselling contract.

If, at assessment, it becomes clear that the other health professional does not know of the approach to a counsellor then there should be no agreement to work together until it is certain the other professional knows and agrees that counselling would be helpful. If there is no agreement then it would be quite wrong to work with the potential client.

Similarly, working with a client who is already in a counselling relationship with another counsellor is rarely a good idea and it should never be done if the current counsellor is unaware that an approach has been made to a new counsellor. There are a number of reasons for this. First, it is unprofessional to treat a colleague in this way; in effect one is stealing a client. Second, however difficult a relationship is it is better for both counsellor and client not to avoid an ending and to finish it, preferably face to face, but if not, by letter. Third, the client may be thinking of changing because of dissatisfaction and has not spoken of it because of fear of recrimination. Both this thought and feeling could be a transference or a projection and this can only be discovered by exploration with the current counsellor. An example of transference could be a fear of rejection by the counsellor. The rejection is circumvented and pre-empted by leaving and finding a new therapist. This could all be an acting out of childhood fears with the new therapist standing in for new and possibly better 'parents'. An example of projection could be the client's repressed and denied anger projected onto the counsellor who is then seen as punitive. The client then fears that the counsellor will be punitive should negative feelings and thoughts be expressed. If there is unexpressed negative transference and the client can be helped and encouraged to speak it, and also understand that seeking a new counsellor was an expression of these negative feelings, then there will be some resolution and an important piece of work done.

Of course there are times when dissatisfaction and fear are not transferential feelings but reality. An example of dissatisfaction would be where the work is blocked owing to unrecognized inexperience or incompetence on the part of the counsellor and an example of fear where the current counsellor is abusing the client. In the first instance it would again be important to insist that the potential client returns to the current counsellor and discusses the feeling that the work is blocked. If a counsellor is well supervised and honest with himself then the truth of what the client is saying should be recognized, and an ending and the help to move to a more experienced counsellor can be negotiated. If this is not the case the client can insist on ending and if the counsellor did oppose this then a BAC *Code of Ethics and Practice* (1997: B.2.2 and B.4.3.2) is being contravened and the client can lodge a complaint.

In the other example, where the current counsellor is abusive, the client may be too frightened to return. This would have to be respected and the client encouraged at least to write a letter to finish the current relationship and also advised about the procedure for lodging a complaint if there is evidence of abuse. The potential counsellor would also have to decide whether there is a duty to confront the current counsellor and, depending on the response, consider lodging a complaint (BAC 1997: B.1.4.2).

Assuming there really are reasons for a client to change counsellors and for an ending to be made face to face or by letter, the potential counsellor needs to discuss the issues at length with a supervisor to decide if they 'should' or 'could' work with this client and if so whether the new counselling relationship should be started immediately. There is no hard and fast rule but it is often wise to suggest a break of one to three months so that the previous work can be consolidated. However, to some clients who are very fragile as a result of the abuse of the previous relationship this would be punitive. Clearly, whether it is decided to start work straight away or with a delay there are likely to be issues that will need to be worked through from the previous relationship. For instance, one difficulty that could arise from the previous counselling relationship is the idealization of the new counsellor as saviour and the vilification of the previous counsellor or vice versa. Except in the case of abuse it is unlikely that either counsellor is as good or as bad as made out by the client. Another example would be an enormous difficulty in trusting the relationship; it is possible even that an existing problem with trust is being exacerbated. As with any other counselling relationship, supervision should help manage the complicated dynamics.

Question 16

Are there ethical as well as practical issues about keeping case-notes?
Roger Casemore

In considering the issues surrounding the keeping of case-notes on counselling clients, it is important to recognize that issues for counsellors working in agencies may be different to those for counsellors working in private practice. There may also be differences, between kinds of agencies or kinds of clientele. However, the BAC *Code of Ethics and Practice for Counsellors* (1997) states, '*Counsellors offer the highest possible levels of confidentiality in order to respect the client's privacy and create the trust necessary for counselling*' (BAC 1997: A.3). This applies to all counsellors no matter what setting they are working in. Unfortunately it does not mean that the information we keep is inviolable and not open to scrutiny by others using whatever means they may have at their disposal. Counsellors and counselling agencies must take responsibility for maintaining the security of information which they hold on clients, and for acquainting themselves with the law in relation to confidentiality, in order to protect themselves and their clients. Jenkins (1997: 12), who is currently the best source of information on this issue, states,

> Confidentiality is one of the first principles that therapists learn on any training course. They quickly go on to discover that this is not necessarily an *absolute* principle, but a guideline which can often be compromised by their professional role, and by organizational considerations, as in the case of social workers working with possible child abuse . . . Confidentiality within therapy is, in reality, enveloped by a much broader concept of the *public interest*. The law sees the benefits of one-to-one confidentiality as potentially outweighed by wider considerations of what is deemed to be in the public interest. Hence the therapist's notes and recollections of sessions can be called into the witness box if need be.

The principal issues in relation to keeping notes are

- Why do we keep them?
- Whose benefit are they for?
- Who should legitimately be able to see them?
- How might they be misused and by whom?
- How do we keep them secure?
- What do we do with them after the client is gone?
- Who deals with them in the event of the death of the therapist?

Why, as a counsellor working in private practice, do I keep notes of my work with a client? Whose benefit is it for? I keep minimum details of each client that help me to identify who they are, and to enable me to contact them if I need to. Name, address and telephone number are usually recorded on a card index or on a computer database, usually with an identifying code number to aid confidentiality regarding this information. Because I am very often inaccurate in guessing someone's age and because it is inappropriate to make assumptions based on preconceptions arising from their appearance, I find it useful to record their date of birth. I also record the details of their GP in case I need to make contact, which I only do with the client's agreement. I list the dates and times of all their appointments with me and of any cancelled appointments, which I often need in order to send invoices, but this also helps in keeping an overview of the case. Finally, if they were referred to me by another professional, I make a note of who referred them because that might at some stage require some contact or feedback. If they were not referred I usually note how they found out about me, which provides some feedback on the effectiveness of my advertising.

That is all the information which I record in the beginning and I keep it in a secure but fairly accessible place. The client is informed about the records that I keep and their entitlement to see these if they wish to. Other counsellors using other therapeutic approaches or working in agency settings may record much more, possibly taking and recording a detailed history of the client and often a diagnostic assessment of their emotional and psychological state. The important issue here is that this is information which the client is likely to regard as appropriate for me to collect and retain, providing that I keep it secure and maintain confidentiality. As a counsellor in private practice, I regard that information as mine, but for a counsellor working in an agency setting the information may be regarded as belonging to the agency, and the agency will determine how it may be treated.

It is important to remember that the Data Protection Act 1998 now covers all recorded information in whatever format, not just that held on computers. Clients have a right to know what information is held on them and to have freedom of access to it. Clearly the capacity to maintain confidentiality of clients' records is of paramount importance and breaches of confidentiality through administrative error, inefficiency or lack of awareness need to be guarded against with vigilance.

Sometimes confidentiality can be breached without our realizing it. I recall my chagrin some years ago, when my financial advisor pointed out to me that my clients' names and addresses appeared on their invoices and the names on their invoices and cheques appeared in my accounts books. These were all seen by him, by my auditors and by the Inland Revenue. I quickly learned to deal with this and to make sure that my clients remained anonymous in my accounts and elsewhere, including on bank paying-in slips.

A far more thorny issue for me is that of taking notes of the therapeutic work with a client as it continues over a period of time. Fortunately I have a good memory, although as I get older, I seem to get the occasional glitch with short-term remembering. In my counselling training I was encouraged to work on developing my memory and my powers of recall and I have continued to do that. As I have never worked with large numbers of clients at any one time, I have never had much trouble in remembering important factual information about them. When I have forgotten things I have never been afraid to check them with the client. Clients seem to have valued that and not expected me to remember everything in detail. I recognize that this may not be the case for others, particularly those working with large case-loads or those working in agencies requiring more detailed informative notes to be kept, and the issue of keeping more detailed information is clearly problematic.

In my training I learned to write brief case-notes as soon as possible after seeing each client and in those notes to focus primarily on how I was experiencing the client, how I was working with them and the process which I observed between us in the therapeutic relationship. I try not to record detailed information about the client's 'story' or information from them which might enable someone else to identify them or those about whom they are talking. Basically I do not put anything in my notes which would be helpful to someone else or potentially harmful to my client. Neither do I put in my notes anything I would not want my client to read, or anything which would prevent me from freely showing my notes to my client.

My notes are not 'privileged' under the law and I could be subpoenaed and required to make them available to the officers of the court. In some cases this could mean that they might be copied and quite widely distributed to the police, solicitors and other parties on both sides. Clearly there is an ethical issue here in deciding what I would do if such a thing were to happen. I could concur and try to negotiate with the court some protective parameters for my notes. I could refuse and have them forcibly taken from me by officers of the court. I could destroy them and suffer the consequences. At one time this might have meant a short spell in prison for contempt of court. However, now that we have lost the right to remain silent it could ultimately lead to a substantial prison sentence.

Another issue arises in relation to the safe keeping of my notes, particularly with the increasing risk of burglary and housebreaking or office-breaking. I need to make sure that I have taken reasonable precautions to protect the information I hold on my clients. First of all, I make clear to my family that a particular filing cabinet is kept locked and must not be touched by them as it contains sensitive, confidential information. I then have to make sure that I sustain an effective defence against the natural curiosity of my children and the temptation that all children have to do precisely the opposite of what they have been told. Second, I need to make sure that in the event of a break-in and theft, my records are as reasonably protected as common sense decrees. I would not want a client suing me because their records had been stolen and circulated around the neighbourhood because I had not protected them adequately.

Another issue which needs to be considered is what precautions I need to take in the event of something untoward happening to me. My records remain confidential even after my death and that confidentiality needs to continue to be protected. It would not be fair for my wife or my executors to be faced with finding and dealing with such sensitive information. I have informed my wife and family where my records are kept and told them about the arrangements for them to be dealt with if something should happen to me. I have included an instruction in my will naming two of my counselling colleagues, so that whichever one is available at the time will take responsibility for destroying all my client case-notes, my client information records and all my notes of my own supervision, along with the notes and records I keep of my supervision of other counsellors and trainee counsellors.

Finally there is the issue of when and how to dispose of my client notes and records. Advice on the length of time that records should be kept varies considerably. BAC's complaints procedure currently allows a complaint to be registered at any time up to five years after the event. The Law Society recommends solicitors to keep client records until six years from the date of last contact, which corresponds with the time limits for some legal actions (see Jenkins 1997, Chapter 6). Both of these points seem to provide good reasons for retaining records for at least that length of time. Doing this may in many cases lead to considerable storage and security problems, and I see no way around that. It is up to each agency and each counsellor to consider that issue in the light of the resources available to them.

There are those in the world of the talking therapies who would say that we are safer not to keep any records at all, on the basis of 'what you haven't got can't be taken from you'. However, if you are going to keep them it would probably be wise to keep them for as long as they are likely to be needed. I suspect most of our clients would prefer us to keep as little information on them as possible and then only to keep what we really need to enable us to work effectively with them. If my basic principles in this context are to enhance my clients' autonomy and to protect their welfare and their privacy, as well as protecting myself, my profession and those close to me, then it is my responsibility to think through all the issues relating to case-notes and to make sure that I have done everything I can to meet those principles.

Question 17

What are the ethical considerations when a former client persists with unwanted contact?
Carol Shillito-Clarke

The kind of relationship that counsellors and psychotherapists have with their clients is, by definition, a formal, contractual one. That the therapeutic relationship will end at some point, whether after one session or several years, is a significant part of the contract and often of the therapeutic work. While some counsellors may establish a different relationship with a client after the therapeutic work has ended, it is not considered usual practice. It also assumes a mutual desire for, and recognition of, the change of relationship by both people, time apart to redress the power balance and some discussion with the therapist's supervisor. Some theoretical orientations consider any different relationship between therapists and their former clients to be highly undesirable.

Ending a relationship, in therapy as in life, can be very difficult, particularly if the relationship has been characterized by a high degree of appreciation, respect and caring. It can be particularly difficult for some clients for whom even a few sessions of therapy may be the first significant experience of a good relationship and whose personal life is still depleted. However, all forms of unwanted contact can be difficult for the recipient. The amount of distress any one counsellor experiences will be dependent on a number of factors. These include the nature of the contact; its frequency, duration and persistence; and the perceived relationship with the client. As the client may have a very different perception driving their behaviour, it is particularly important to establish exactly what 'persisting with unwanted contact' means.

What does 'persisting with unwanted contact' mean?

There is a lot of difference between the client who sends a card every month or so following the end of counselling, and the former client who sits outside the counsellor's home, calls on the telephone several times a day, follows them and pries into their private life. It is important to keep a full and accurate record of the 'contact' as well as the actions that have been taken to stop it; what exactly happens, how often, and whether anyone else is involved.

The counsellor's ethical duty to the client

According to the current BAC code, the counsellor's primary responsibility is to the client, to ensure that she or he comes to no harm. The counsellor is also responsible for ensuring that the ending of the work is appropriate to the client's needs or that the client is referred to another source of help, that the client is treated with respect, that confidentiality is maintained after the end of therapy and that the counsellor promotes the client's autonomy (BAC 1997).

As the first duty is to the client, the counsellor needs to review and consider the whole of the therapy with their supervisor. Counsellors who are working for an organization or agency may also need to inform their line-manager, maintaining appropriate boundaries of confidentiality. The issues that may be important to consider include

- the source of referral, by whom and for what reason and whether other professionals such as the GP or psychiatric services were and still may be involved,
- what is known of any previous experience of therapy and its ending,
- the nature of the therapeutic contract that was offered – the focus of the work, the number of sessions offered and so on,
- the content of the therapy work, particularly if it involved issues of attachment and loss that may make the ending of the therapeutic relationship more difficult,
- the therapeutic process, particularly relating to the client's desire for extended contact with the counsellor and how this was dealt with,
- the reasons for ending the work and whether this was negotiated with the client and
- how the ending was managed, whether a referral on was offered or accepted, whether a 'door was left open' for future return or whether endings were simply not addressed.

In relation to the last point the counsellor needs also to re-examine her or his own feelings about, and competence in, making clear endings. If the ending has been ambiguous, the client may not feel that their needs have been appropriately met and will be willing to stop making contact once this has been recognized.

Addressing the need for a clear ending

The BAC code considers the counsellor's ethical responsibility is to 'work with clients to reach a recognized ending' (BAC 1997: B.1.3.8). It is therefore important to determine how the work was ended and what might be done to resolve the situation ethically, respecting both the needs of the client and the counsellor.

If the counsellor is unable to complete the work with the client, perhaps because of illness or a house move, then the client needs to be helped to accept a referral on to an appropriate source of further help, making it clear that the counsellor is no longer available. If the work was ended because of some organizational circumstance such as a limited number of sessions, then the counsellor needs to renegotiate the contract both with their organization and with the client, allowing for a specific number of sessions with the agreed focus on ending. Similarly, if the counsellor misjudged the client's need of the therapeutic relationship, a further, limited contract to make a clear and suitable ending may be necessary. If the 'door' was 'left open' it needs to be respectfully and firmly shut.

It is important to remember that, for the client with difficulties around attachment and separation, any form of contact with the counsellor is going to restimulate feeling, therefore the use of an intermediary may be important.

If the counsellor is confident that an unambiguous and clear ending was made and that the client's needs were appropriately respected and addressed, then it becomes important to perceive the client's attentions as a form of harassment and possibly stalking. Therapists who work from home are more vulnerable to harassment and need to be alert to the potential when selecting clients. The maintenance of firm, clear boundaries is particularly important.

Psychologists at Manchester Metropolitan University are currently researching the stalking of therapists and counsellors, which they believe may be an under-reported problem. Stalkers are described as people, often known to psychiatric and forensic services, with histories of failed and disturbed relationships who are very controlling and emotionally abusive. The motivation for stalking is usually anger and control rather than sex or love (Holmes *et al.* 2000).

While the counsellor has an ethical duty to protect himself or herself from physical harm there is no statement in the current BAC codes that they may act to protect themselves from psychological harm such as might arise from being stalked. The Protection from Harassment Act 1997 covers stalking but the counsellor should take advice from their professional body and insurance company in order to be very clear about their legal position in this respect. As Holmes *et al.* point out, the use of legal proceedings can, paradoxically, further the stalker's aim of contact with the therapist rather than protect them.

Question 18

How might the ethical issues when counselling children and young people be different from when working with adults?
Roger Casemore

Article 12 of the United Nations Convention on the Rights of the Child (1999) requires each member state to ensure

- that any child capable of forming a view has the right to express views freely in all matters affecting him or her and
- that the child's views are given due weight in accordance with age and maturity.

It also states that these rights underline children's status

- as individuals with fundamental rights and feelings of their own,
- with a right to involvement in decision-making about matters which affect them.

Children are people and while they need to be valued equally with other people, they also need to be valued for their difference as children from adults. This is not only because there are some intrinsic differences between being a child and being an adult but also because they experience the world we all share differently from adults.

There are significant differences between children and adults in their capacity to think and to make sense of their world and their experiences. Erikson (1959) suggested that a continuing concern for the developing individual is the struggle between the continuing drive to develop a self-identity which is in conflict with the continuing experience of role-confusion. The capacity to come to terms with the existence of this polarity requires the developing child to become capable of dialectical thought. Erikson's research suggested that the child's capacity to think dialectically and accept the existence of two truths does not appear to develop until quite late in adolescence. In their research, Gilligan and Murphy (1979) found that the capacity of children and adolescents for moral reasoning is too simplistic and that only in early adulthood do they develop the capacity to reunite abstract ideas with the concrete reality of their experience and to be able to develop more complex forms of reasoning. Riegel (1979) suggested that dialectical thought can only be achieved by the mature adult who has developed the capacity to comprehend contradictions. Before adulthood, individuals generally tend to see the world in very stark terms with few and limited choices in dealing with dilemmas. In working as a counsellor with children and adolescents, I have an ethical responsibility to value the differences between them and my adult clients and to take account of their intellectual capacity to resolve the problems and concerns with which they are faced.

In counselling adults I am clear about my ethical responsibilities towards my clients, all of whom I regard as autonomous individuals with considerable freedom within the law to choose what they say and what they do. I have an understanding of their rights as individuals in society and their responsibilities for the consequences of their decisions and their actions. It is probably only when my clients begin to disclose that they have committed or are considering committing serious criminal offences, or are considering suicide or other forms of harm to themselves, that I am really faced with ethical dilemmas. Usually, most of my ethical dilemmas in counselling are concerned with ensuring that I behave ethically towards my clients, treating them with respect and honesty, working always towards their benefit by enhancing their autonomy, maintaining strict confidentiality and ensuring the highest levels of my own competence in my work with them.

In working with children and young people, I would suggest that there are different ethical considerations which may affect the practice of counsellors. These considerations would be likely to occur under three of the generally agreed principal ethical dimensions of 'autonomy', 'confidentiality' and 'competence'. While in general terms a counsellor would be expected to ensure that the same ethical principles underpin all their therapeutic work, there may be some variations to the application of these principles in working with young people, arising from the different legal status of children and young people and their position in society.

It is particularly important to recognize that all counsellors have an ethical responsibility in relation to the law. The BAC *Code of Ethics and Practice for Counsellors* originally stated that *'counsellors should work within the law'* (BAC 1990 and 1993). The current code states only that counsellors should *'be aware of the law'* (BAC 1997: B.1.6.1). This perhaps takes account of the well-known legal principle that ignorance of the law is no defence. However, it may well be that, in working with children and young people, there are a number of situations where compliance with the law could contradict ethical considerations and vice versa, presenting counsellors with significant dilemmas to resolve and putting them and their clients at some risk. For example, while all counsellors abide by the principle of working to enable their clients to maximize the client's autonomy, the legal position in relation to children and young people places clear limitations on this. There are a number of ways in which at certain ages the autonomy of children and young people is limited in comparison to that of adults and this can be particularly problematic for those working with young people in schools, social-work settings and youth-work settings. Young people's freedom of choice and action is variously limited by the law in relation to a number of activities including smoking, drinking alcohol, consent to sexual activity, leaving home, attending school, driving, insurance and finance to name but a few. This lack of freedom and reduced autonomy of the child or young person can present real ethical problems to the counsellor working in confidence with them to enable them to become more resourceful and to live a more satisfying life. Certainly I would suggest that counsellors should keep themselves well informed of the legal rights and freedoms of children and young people in order to be fully aware of the constraints on their client's autonomy and to consider how best they can work within those constraints.

Counsellors working hard to abide by the ethical principle of confidentiality may well find significant ethical difficulties in offering counselling to children and young people. For example, there can be real conflicts between the law and counselling ethics in relation to a child disclosing information about abuse to a counsellor. Those counsellors working in schools, social work or other agency settings may be legally obliged to pass on that information instantly, in order to instigate action to protect the child and deal with the perpetrator. They may have no freedom to refrain from doing that and very little freedom to delay taking such action, even though in their view it may benefit the child to do so and is ethically appropriate. Counsellors working in private practice may have a little more freedom to take their time in conveying that information to the proper authorities or even the freedom to determine that they are under no legal obligation to do so, if it is to the client's benefit to withhold the information, but this in itself presents an ethical dilemma which might be different when working with an adult.

Within the ethical principle of confidentiality that most of us hold is the belief that clients should have the right to choose to come to counselling, to choose their counsellor and for the existence of the relationship to be treated as confidential along with any information that is disclosed in the relationship. In a number of contexts either the law or organizational regulations militate against keeping to that ethical principle. In many schools parents' permission has to be sought before a child can see a counsellor, senior staff may demand to know the names of children seeing the counsellor and it is still not uncommon for children to be sent to the school counsellor for misbehaviour. The counsellor may also have a legal obligation, under the terms of their employment, to breach confidentiality and inform the headteacher of disclosures made by a child, and these need not necessarily be just in relation to disclosures of child abuse. Further useful information on this can be found in the *Counselling in Education: Guidelines on Counselling in Schools* (BAC 1998c) and in *Confidentiality and School Counselling – Occasional Paper Number 1* (Casemore 1995).

Much is written elsewhere about the law in relation to the rights of children and young people and this chapter is not the place to enter into that detail. The National Youth Agency in Leicester (telephone 0116 285 3700 fax 0116 285 3777) has a substantial free Information Service on all matters relating to young people and the Department for Education and Employment (telephone 0207 273 6339) is a further useful source of information and advice.

In relation to the third ethical principle of competence, which I mentioned above, it may not be clear how this might be breached. Some counsellors may well consider that working with children is no different to working with adults, that the skills and processes which they use are the same regardless of age, and see no need to ensure that they have different competences for working with children and young people. Most of us working with children and young people would heartily challenge that view and would suggest that working with them calls for different knowledge, different skills and expertise and some variation in approach to that used in working with adults, not least for some of the reasons stated in the opening paragraph above. In particular it calls for a real understanding of how young people experience their world and their position in it. It is therefore an ethical requirement that counsellors wanting to work with children and young people should seek some additional training and professional development and should also consider the nature of the supervision they require for this work. In my case, I take my clinical work with children and young people to a supervisor who also has experience of that kind of work and can really understand the context of what I am presenting for supervision. It seems to me that it would be unethical of me to do otherwise.

Question 19

What are my responsibilities when I suspect another counsellor is behaving unethically?
Caroline Jones

Counsellors who suspect another of unethical behaviour have to consider moral and ethical responsibilities. Unethical behaviour includes

- breaching professional codes of ethics when working with clients whether accidentally, deliberately or through negligence,
- acting in ways that cause harm to clients and
- undermining public confidence in counselling more generally through misconduct.

Weighing up whether to take some action, either personally or by passing on any suspicions to those who are formally obliged to pursue such matters, contributes to safeguarding ethical standards in client work and the credibility of counselling. I have identified up to four steps to take:

- assessing the nature and seriousness of the possible unethical conduct,
- approaching the suspected counsellor informally to discuss the matter,

- contacting any relevant bodies such as professional association(s) or employers informally and
- if appropriate, making a formal complaint.

The allegations of unethical behaviour may be of such a profoundly serious nature that making a formal complaint is the only option.

When counsellors are in the same professional association, there is normally no choice but to take some action in serious instances, as many organizations (AHPP, BAC, BPS, COSCA and UKCP for example) place this obligation on their membership. BAC's guidance to its membership on this question states that 'counsellors must not conduct themselves in their counselling-related activities in ways which undermine public confidence either in their role as a counsellor or in the work of other counsellors' and suggests the necessary steps that should be taken. Unethical behaviour must always be taken seriously although this does not always require recourse to a formal complaints procedure. I would like to illustrate this by using counsellor sleepiness during sessions as an example.

A counsellor might start to doze on one occasion as a consequence of taking a cold remedy before work that day, explain and apologize to the client immediately (a mistake). Another counsellor whose functioning is affected by a medical or other condition might regularly fall asleep while working with clients but refuse to take the necessary steps to avoid this happening (malpractice). Another counsellor may start dozing as a result of a series of late nights or tiredness from booking too many appointments that day (poor practice). Another may sometimes experience tiredness to the point of dozing within sessions when working with particular clients where unexpressed powerful negative emotions may be present; this is a separate and recognizable therapeutic issue that a counsellor should respond to appropriately. Allowing this to happen repeatedly without recognizing and understanding its significance could indicate poor practice or be an example of working beyond one's competence (negligence or malpractice). Counsellor sleepiness can therefore be categorized in various ways.

Assessing the nature of the possible unethical conduct and any evidence of this, the first step indicated earlier, may be straightforward or involve its own dilemmas. Others rarely witness an individual counsellor's work with a client, so direct evidence of breaches of codes, or of causing harm to clients, is not easily obtained. Other kinds of unethical behaviour, such as a disrespectful way of discussing clients, either in counselling supervision or training contexts, or breaches of confidentiality or inaccurate advertising, are more easily evidenced and thus taking action is more straightforward. Occasionally a client may talk about a previous therapist and their behaviour. The current counsellor is faced with a dilemma here, receiving information of a possible breach of ethics and unsure whether the client understands the seriousness of this. The client may not be aware that a complaint could be brought against the offending counsellor, or if they are aware, they may choose not to pursue this. The client has a right to self-determination in this matter, based on all available information. This includes the relevant codes required to understand the standards expected and details of where help is available, such as the Prevention of Professional Abuse Network (POPAN) listed in Appendix 2. Meanwhile the counsellor possesses information about the possible unethical practice of another and is bound by confidentiality while concerned that other clients could also be at risk. The counsellor is also alert to another possibility: that the client is trying to put right something in the current therapeutic relationship and looking for the opportunity to talk through any concerns more directly.

That the first-hand evidence of clients is often necessary in order to lodge a complaint poses one of the more difficult ethical dilemmas for counsellors. Any encouragement to a current client to pursue a complaint against a former therapist could in itself be unethical as it could appear abusive and exploitative. Balancing what does the greatest good and what does the least harm is a difficult choice in these circumstances.

Approaching the suspected counsellor informally to discuss the matter is a possible option. Even when faced with information given in confidence, a counsellor might find a way of approaching another to discuss suspected unethical behaviour. It is likely to be a difficult meeting and adequate preparation is essential. This task requires attention to the values of counselling (integrity, impartiality and respect) by the concerned counsellor. Taking notes before, during and after the meeting is a sensible precaution for the counsellor initiating the meeting, so that subsequent reflection is based on as accurate as possible a record of the discussion. The reflections will involve considering how the suspected counsellor reacted to the concerns. This may appear a subjective way to proceed but is an important consideration. Counsellors sometimes make mistakes and acknowledging these is a part of the learning process. BAC's code (1997: B.1.5.1) is a useful tool in these circumstances, as it obliges members to be accountable to colleagues. More than one meeting may be necessary to reach a satisfactory outcome and employing the services of a mediator might assist towards a satisfactory outcome.

Approaching the appropriate professional association(s) and other bodies informally is another possible step. At this stage, whether the suspected counsellor has already been approached or not, the concerned counsellor will probably want to consult others – in confidence. This is a step that can be taken by simply stating that there are concerns about a particular counsellor's practice.

Making a formal complaint is the ultimate step and a difficult one for all concerned as complaints procedures, once invoked, normally continue to a conclusion and it can take time for a formal complaint to be processed. Having made a formal complaint, the concerned counsellor knows that the matter is now the responsibility of the professional association(s). One benefit of making a formal complaint is that this can be investigated and adjudicated by practitioners who have experience in the setting and with the theoretical approach of the member complained against. This expertise may be necessary to achieve natural justice. There are occasions when counsellors dislike or disapprove of aspects of practice by others although this does not necessarily mean that such practice is unethical.

It may seem relatively straightforward to set out these steps and give the impression that the whole matter can be dealt with in a rational and dispassionate way. In reality, it can be an unwelcome experience for all concerned. Equally difficult are the occasions when my own practice is below standard. Recognizing, acknowledging and dealing with instances of my own mistakes or faulty judgements are my ongoing responsibilities and keep me alert and humble. My codes give an ethical framework to my work, telling me what I must and must not do and what I should and should not do but these do not cover all eventualities within a counselling relationship. Having the right counselling supervisor, someone with whom I feel safe to explore my client work openly and honestly, is an essential safeguard for my clients. The development of my 'internal supervisor' (Casement 1985) is another essential element of mature and ethical practice. Other general requirements of reflective and ethical practice include continuing professional development, the process of applying for and maintaining registration (accreditation), reading and other ways of learning both from the best practice of others and from their mistakes. Most of all, I have to keep open to learning from clients.

Safeguarding clients from unethical practice can also be facilitated by assisting clients in their understanding of ethics in counselling. Proffering copies of the *Basic Principles of Counselling* (BAC 1991), as part of pre-counselling information and when contracting, is good practice. This is a particularly useful document, encapsulating in ten points the key information clients need to know. It is through openness with clients about how we define ethics in counselling and therapy that the profession can offer the best protection against unethical behaviour.

In conclusion, available evidence in professional journals shows that the numbers of formal complaints that are upheld are low in proportion to the numbers of practising counsellors. Formal complaints range from one-off mistakes to malpractice and the sanctions imposed reflect this. The most serious sanction that any professional association can currently impose is expulsion. As yet, no one can be prevented from working as a counsellor. Literature from POPAN illustrates the harm resulting from abuse by members of a number of professions, including counsellors and therapists, and reinforces our duty to be vigilant about our own practice and that of others.

SECTION 3

Ethics in training and continuing professional development

Question 20

A trainer has a reputation for covert discriminatory practice but this is apparently unchallenged. Whose responsibility is this and how should it be addressed?
Carol Shillito-Clarke

Discriminatory behaviour means the singling out of a person or a group of people for special attention on the basis of some perceived difference which is valued either positively or negatively. Such perceived differences include race, gender, class, religion, age, mental and physical ability, sexual preference and economic status. The problem lies not with the perception of difference but with the way in which the difference is valued, consciously and unconsciously, and how that affects the behaviour of those who share the perception towards those who are 'different'. Most social discrimination is negative in that the target person or group is perceived to be of lesser status and value to the perceiver and therefore less worthy of respectful attention and behaviour. Positive discrimination is usually invoked to counter situations where there is negative discrimination.

In counselling and therapy, any form of negative discrimination or oppressive behaviour is considered to be unethical because it insults the person or persons involved and contravenes the values of integrity, impartiality and respect (Davies and Neal 1996; Kearney 1996; Lago and Thompson 1996; BAC 1997; BPS DCoP 1998; UKCP

1998). In addition, discrimination by a trainer is unacceptable because it abuses the power of the training role, models unethical practice and makes it difficult for students to learn more about their own attitudes and values. It also harms the public image of counselling. Not only is discriminatory behaviour by a trainer unethical in the eyes of any therapeutic body such as BAC, UKCP or BPS, it should also be condemned by any reputable training institution and may have legal consequences.

The question as posed, however, is rather vague and this may be a nice reflection of the difficulties inherent in such a situation. Before any action is taken a number of points need to be clarified.

What is the nature of this 'reputation' and who holds it?

A reputation held among a group of students on a course is a different matter from a reputation that is held by the local therapeutic community. A particular group of students may hold perceptions about a trainer that arise out of the group dynamic and are neither supported by previous or subsequent groups nor endure beyond a relatively short time span. A trainer's reputation for poor practice or behaviour, held in the local community, is less easy to control, refute or substantiate. It can therefore last longer and be more damaging to the trainer, students, course and institution.

What is the behaviour that is considered discriminatory and what is meant by 'covert'?

The term 'covert discrimination' may cover a wide range of possibilities. It is important to establish what exactly the discriminatory behaviour is perceived to be; against whom; and the severity, frequency and duration of its incidence. There is a difference in the degree of seriousness between an occasional insensitive joke or lack of recognition of a minority interest, and a regular, ongoing bias towards one person or group over another that perhaps affects course material or assessment criteria.

What is meant by 'apparently unchallenged'?

What is known of the history of the alleged discriminatory practice, its origins and any previous attempts to address it? Again, there is a significant difference between someone being confronted or charged with unethical behaviour which they continue to exhibit, and someone being unaware that what they are doing is unacceptable to others. If the behaviour has never been challenged it is important to consider why. Such a lack of challenge may reveal something about a group of colleagues, course or institution.

What evidence is there to support the concern?

The issue of evidence is critically important here. Without clear, reliable, first-hand, documented evidence there can be no charge to answer. As Palmer Barnes states, 'The more serious the offence, the more thoroughly and unambiguously it needs to be proved' (Palmer Barnes 1998: 59). If evidence can be put together to demonstrate that the trainer is behaving in a discriminatory way then the matter can be dealt with properly. Until such time, any counsellors hearing a rumour should themselves behave ethically. Rather than promote it further they should underline that it is currently without foundation. Considerable distress, if not psychological harm, may be caused to the person complained about, even if they are subsequently found to be not guilty.

Who is responsible for addressing the problem?

Discriminatory behaviour is against the law. Managers have a duty to ensure that such behaviour does not occur in their organizations. Counsellors and trainers, who are members of a professional body, are considered to be ethically responsible for the promotion of appropriate standards of practice both by themselves and by others (BAC 1997; BPS 1998; UKCP 1998). Students or staff who are individual members of BAC, or members of a course that is an organizational member, are ethically responsible not to allow rumours of discriminatory behaviour to continue unchallenged (BAC 1996b).

How should the problem be addressed?

First, the person or people considering taking some action against the trainer should, if possible, discuss it with another professional who is sufficiently informed and objective to be able to offer them appropriate guidance and support. It must be remembered that in any discussions, issues of confidentiality need to be given careful consideration and information shared only on a 'need-to-know' basis.

The BAC *Code of Ethics and Practice for Counsellors* requires that all members of the association have a responsibility to address acts of misconduct by other members (BAC 1997). Anyone who has evidence that a trainer is behaving in a discriminatory way has a duty to approach the trainer directly, present them with the evidence, clarify its validity and ask them to change. While this is easy to recommend it needs to be realized that it takes a lot of courage for a student or group of students to challenge the authority and power of a trainer. Students may feel they are putting their qualifications at risk. Despite the ethical responsibility, teaching colleagues may also find a personal approach difficult, particularly if they have an ongoing working relationship or even a friendship with the trainer. Any member of the training community complaining about another member risks discrimination by management, other members of the staff or the student body. This is particularly likely if the person complained about is a prominent member of the profession, a senior member of the organization or a charismatic leader. The complainant may be misperceived as a troublemaker, be denigrated and labelled as having problems with authority figures, or be considered merely personally vindictive towards the trainer. However, trainers also have an ethical duty to respect the experiences of their trainees (*Code of Ethics and Practice for Trainers*, BAC 1996b).

If a personal approach fails to achieve any results and there is evidence that the discriminatory behaviour is continuing, the next option is to institute a grievance procedure with the institution. Should the institution be one that is managed by fear and corruption, or by lack of care for appropriate standards, Palmer Barnes suggests that it may not be safe for the complainant to use the institution's procedures. Instead the complainant should approach the trainer's professional body directly, assuming he or she is a member of one (Palmer Barnes 1998).

The trainer should be informed immediately of any grievance procedure or complaint that is being brought. A meeting with all the relevant parties can then be called as soon as possible. The first meeting between the trainer and those complaining about the trainer's behaviour needs to be conducted in a non-threatening manner in keeping with the counselling ethos of integrity, impartiality and respect. The aim of such a meeting would be to reappraise the trainer of the complainant's perceptions of their behaviour and enable all parties to discuss the concerns and the evidence for it. The trainer needs to have sufficient information to be able to explore and review their practice and recognize the distress caused. He or she also needs to be given the opportunity to apologize and make the necessary changes.

If the charges are denied or if there is no subsequent change in the perceived behaviour then further steps will need to be taken. These may be clearly set out by the organization for which the trainer is working. The authority to whom the complaint is addressed will depend on the kind of organization within which the training is taking place. If the trainer is a member of a professional body, they may become involved if the matter cannot be resolved internally. As these are serious matters with potential long-term effects on the careers of those involved, it is important that all meetings are carefully minuted and copies of these and any written communications between the various parties kept on file.

Discriminatory behaviour by trainers, as by any member of the therapeutic body, is unethical. It damages individuals and harms the reputation of the course and the profession. Under certain circumstances, it may also be illegal. Because it is such a serious matter, it is ethically important that any such situation is thoroughly investigated so that it may be shown either that the rumour is unfounded or that there is sufficient evidence to support it. In this event it is incumbent on the parties to demonstrate that all avenues to resolving the situation have been explored before formal complaints procedures are invoked.

Question 21

The theoretical underpinnings of much couple therapy are based on Western thought and the central importance given to the individual, to autonomy and to an expectation that what we call intimate relationships can be conducted in private. The UK now contains many ethnic minorities for whom these ideas are in conflict with their cultural

norms. Is it ethical to train counsellors on the basis of Western thought alone?
Derek Hill

This question prompts several others:

- Is it ethical to offer (couple) counselling which expresses a cultural bias?
- What are the essential features of *couple* counselling?
- What constitutes an effective professional training in couple counselling?
- What effect does the theoretical underpinning of couple counselling have on its process and outcomes and thus on the clients' experience of it?

These subsidiary questions do not identify mutually exclusive issues but their consideration will help to tease out an ethical and practical answer to the dilemma that has been posed.

Cultural bias

The expression of a culture, and the beliefs, attitudes, values and meanings on which it is based, is achieved through social institutions and policies, the forms and content of its creative life, patterns of communal life, structured interpersonal behaviour, language and gesture. The central role of language and gesture in the 'talking cures' results in their processes being, among other things, dialogues within or between cultures. English language-medium counselling inevitably traffics in meanings that reflect its complex societal origins. That complexity contributes to the language's richness but does not rid it of bias. The continuing debate about what Freud actually meant in his writings illustrates the fact that different languages speak of different world-views even within Europe. Ideas expressed in Cantonese have a coloration which can never be completely captured in English. Cultural bias is thus built into the talking cures.

The ethical issue faced by counselling is how it deals with that inherent bias. It can creatively exploit it through mother-tongue counselling services. At the other extreme, it can wittingly or unwittingly employ it as an oppressive and discriminatory influence. Institutionally, this might occur where no language-medium options are offered to clients. An individual practitioner might fall into the trap if no deviation is allowed from his or her world-view and meanings. This last example draws attention to the fact that the world's major languages have the capacity to express different philosophies and theoretical orientations. While limited to working in English a counsellor might express post-Freudian, postmodern or Taoist ideas.

A remarkable undertaking is in progress in New Zealand which involves NZAC (the New Zealand Association of Counsellors) and the Maori Association, Te Whariki Tautoko, which have joined forces to ensure that both culturally specific mother-tongue counselling and cross-cultural counselling are available (Syme 1999). Organizations such as Relate in England are learning important lessons from professional dialogue with colleagues in that country.

The core issue is the management of the culturally biased means of communication we are all compelled to use. It can exacerbate power differences between counsellor and client, or be employed as the imperfect means by which to learn about, respect and value lives being lived with a different perspective. In this context it is salutary to reflect on the findings of experiments in which people seek, temporarily, to experience the daily life of those with different faculties or physical capacities, such as visual impairment. The contrasting experiences thus gained can enrich awareness and understanding of others and of self. Finishing a session with clients with a powerful sense of having deepened self-understanding is a commonplace experience for many counsellors, and an affirmation of the mutually transforming nature of the process in which they have been involved.

Counsellors and their clients manifest their cultural affiliations in every word and gesture but if care is taken not to abuse power (BAC 1997: B.1.3.4), and genuine efforts are made to respect and promote clients' ability to make decisions in the light of their own beliefs, values and context (BAC 1997: B.2.2), the process in which they engage can be both ethical and mutually rewarding.

Couple counselling

Couple relationships are essentially an amalgam of shared attributes, expectations and aspirations, accommodated differences, and a continuing process of adjustment and problem-solving as the relationship's context, and the partners themselves, change. Couple counselling, with the relationship as client, provides help for those processes of adjustment and problem-solving and is arguably the form of counselling in which issues about similarities and differences are most clearly present in the room, sharply defined and preoccupying. Couple counsellors employ sensitivities to the nature and needs of the partners' evolving 'fit' in terms of socio-cultural affiliations, personal norms, and inter- and intra-psychic dynamics (Dicks 1967). Making a place for, respecting and working with differences lies at the heart of the work.

Effective couple counsellor training

Faced with the uniqueness of every couple relationship, the great range of cultures to which partners may be affiliated, and the growing variety of forms and functions couple relationships may have within their societies, it is almost inevitable that couple counsellor training is informed by the thought that the couple are the experts on their relationship. An effective training must develop (self-)awareness, couple counselling skills and some coherent conceptual framework within which to hypothesize about human development, change and relationships. It must also equip the practitioner with a practised readiness, and the dexterity with ideas and language, to work within the clients' assumptive framework(s). This enables the clients to make informed decisions, and to undertake problem-solving on the basis of their own experience, beliefs, values and meanings. This last requirement prompts the practitioner's development of the skills to create and work with 'moving metaphors' (Hobson 1985: 55) and thus the capacity to compare and contrast the dissimilar. It also opens a door to postmodern narrative work through which clients can evolve new stories about themselves by tapping into their own and others' experiences of relationships and roles, and into the multi-cultural resources of their society (McLeod 1997: 137).

There is a fundamental requirement of any such training: it must offer the trainees the experience of becoming more and more the expert about themselves and about their own roles and relationships. That process is probably best achieved by making use of philosophical principles and theoretical frameworks drawn from their own cultures and communities. That self-knowledge is the 'secure base' (Bowlby 1988) from which they will venture into the worlds and stories of their clients. Those journeyings will be undertaken with the intention of consolidating clients' expertise in living meaningful lives, but with the expectation that the process will have the rewarding, mutually transforming quality mentioned earlier.

The impact of the practitioner's theories on the clients' experience of counselling

At one extreme, clients may seek, and experience, an induction into a particular therapeutic approach and its cultural heritage – a sort of 'training analysis' – and that induction can be soundly rooted in ethical principles. At the other extreme, clients may seek a 'like-minded' practitioner whose function will be, among other things, the consolidation of beliefs, values and meanings already possessed by the clients. This too can be an ethical process, the proviso being that the culture underpinned is living and lively. Between those extremes lies the therapeutic territory that has been mapped earlier. Just as every couple relationship is unique, so every counselling intervention is a unique process made out of the contributions of those involved. Potentially, it is a celebration of the unique qualities of each of the persons involved. Each of the participants has their own starting place and each should have the option to draw on the experiences, beliefs and values of the others as they work together to characterize and value the couple relationship, and explore the options for its future development. Couple counselling focuses attention on the question of whether the partners are able to evolve stories about themselves as individuals which are mutually acceptable, and stories about their relationship which are compatible and hold the promise of the rewards of shared lives.

Couple counselling would progress towards its goal most directly if all involved were totally conversant with each other's experiences and cultures, but that is never true. It is the counsellor's task to create an environment in which all involved are ready to acknowledge their starting places and willing to share in the task of finding the language, the ideas and the creative metaphors which can bridge the gulfs between them. If this can be done, with a close attention to the potentially destructive influence of power differentials, the ethical issue is not to do with the practitioner's philosophical and theoretical affiliations, but with their capacity and willingness to learn about, work within, and learn from dissimilar frames of reference.

Conclusion

It is doubtful whether training couple counsellors on the basis of Western thought alone is a practical proposition. The direct and indirect influences of other cultures pervade psychotherapeutic thinking. Jung alone is a significant influence in this respect. Today, it is increasingly probable that the individual will train alongside, or be trained by, others with different, non-Western cultural heritages, and so be exposed to contrasting value systems and conceptual frameworks. In addition to those influences, couple counseller training has been described as essentially to do with learning to respect and work within several cultural contexts, be they those of different households in Dorchester, or of partners from Dakar and Derby. These practical considerations have important implications for couple counsellor training organizations and their trainers. Cultural interchange depends on the careful management of the power differentials between all those involved and calls on them to pay particular attention to the core values of counselling – integrity, impartiality and respect.

It is not ethical to seek to train couple counsellors to value Western philosophies and thought alone, but then it is highly improbable that this is ever done. It is wise and respectful to encourage trainees to put the thinking of their own culture at the centre of the work they do to acquire competence as couple counsellors, but only because when they are secure and insightful about their own identity they will be free to take the second step, that of moving between and inhabiting a couple's worlds.

Question 22

Is it ethical to give clients to new trainees and should trainees have their clients chosen for them?
Lesley Murdin

From the trainee's point of view the dilemma is more a practical problem: 'how do I get experience of counselling when I have no experience of counselling? How do I find a placement and begin to see clients before I am qualified to do so? If I don't see clients, how can I become qualified to see them?' Trainees are obliged in counselling and psychotherapy courses of any value to have supervised casework experience. Trainees will naturally seek experience whether it is appropriate for them or not and the responsibility for this rests with the training course.

As someone responsible for running training courses, I see two main areas of ethical responsibility which are sometimes in conflict.

On the one hand, my paramount responsibility is to the clients who come for therapy. On the other hand, I have a responsibility to those who come for training in counselling or psychotherapy. They need experience with clients. How else can they learn what is neither an art nor a science but a craft requiring, essentially, an apprenticeship? We need to allocate clients to trainees knowing that they are naïve and inexperienced and sometimes, as for example in GP practices, knowing that the trainee may be taking work that could be done professionally by qualified therapists. If we seek placements for trainees we could be said to be colluding in supplying cheap unqualified labour.

In the vast majority of cases where trainees see clients, all is well from the client's point of view. Trainee therapists are often extremely conscientious and hard-working. We make sure that they have excellent and intensive supervision. Research has so far indicated that clients do at least as well with trainees as with more experienced therapists in terms of the outcomes that they report (Macdonald 1992). Occasionally there are difficulties.

A new trainee, Marilyn reaches the stage where the agency in which she is training would normally allocate a client to her. She has had a year's preparatory course in which she learnt facilitative and empathic listening and responding skills. She has done some voluntary befriending work in an old people's home. She has done well enough to receive a positive reference to continue into the current stage of training in which she will actually see clients. She is asked to see a client whose mother died a year ago and who is suffering from sufficiently severe depression to have taken time off work. The client also has difficulties with her partner who is fed up with her misery.

Marilyn is delighted to be about to see a client, but she comes to supervision after the first session crestfallen. The client told her story with a good deal of hesitation and then at the very end said that she did not think that she would come any more and left. After examining what happened, the supervisor encourages Marilyn, pointing out that some people are just not ready for counselling or not able to delve any deeper into their distress. She is allocated another client who has suffered a series of relationships that have all ended unhappily. The same thing happens: the client comes and leaves at the end of one session. The supervisor then has to decide, is it Marilyn? Should more clients be allocated to her because she has just been unlucky in these two, or is she doing something to drive them away? Her responses seem to be appropriate although she says that she felt very nervous. The only thing that the supervisor has noticed is that Marilyn seems very anxious when talking about the clients' losses and in fact at one point moved the client away from distress with the question 'what else have you found difficult recently?'. As a result the supervisor asks to see Marilyn separately. She asks what her own experience of loss has been and after some prevarication Marilyn acknowledges that she has lost a child who died in an accident three years before. The outcome is that she is advised to continue in her own therapy but take time out from the counselling training until she thinks that she is able to cope. She disagrees strongly with this moratorium, saying that she is perfectly capable of dealing with loss and that these two clients were just difficult.

This is a fictional situation but it represents the kind of problem that may arise with someone who is seeing clients whose difficulties resonate with their own. This obviously applies to all therapists, not just new trainees. There is, however, a particular problem in that those who are allocating clients have some responsibility to make the best judgement possible. Asherst (1993) stresses her wish to assess all the clients for trainees that she supervises. A major bereavement, the loss of a partner or a child, is likely to be a contraindication for anyone, even the very experienced. A new trainee is untested and lacking in the professional experience that teaches us to set aside our personal difficulties to some extent when working.

Most training courses carry out their ethical responsibilities to clients in several ways. The first and in my view the most important is in selecting trainees who are interviewed with a view to discovering that they are stable enough, responsive and self-aware. One of the most important questions to pose to interviewers when they see applicants is 'would you be willing to talk to this person if you were a client?'.

Second, in addition to the rigour of the selection procedure, there is the safeguard provided by personal therapy. Although clearly this does not ensure that there will never be problems as in the case described above, it does mean that there is someone to look after the trainee if the unpleasant decision to delay or terminate client work had to be made. It also means that the trainee's own personal involvement, for example in loss, may be understood and may therefore never interfere as grossly as in the example above.

The trainee who takes on cases that are too demanding for his or her own sensitivity is at one end of the spectrum. The over-anxious trainee is at the other end. Such a trainee may look at the notes on the assessment of a client and decline to take on the case, as in the following example.

Janet was to begin work with her first new client. Her supervisor found a client who had been assessed by an experienced therapist as was usual in the agency. The client was a man who had hit his female partner and wanted to work on better control of anger. Janet read the notes and said that she did not think that she could work well with this client. She said that she had had difficult experiences with violent men and would not like to see a man, especially one with a violent history. The supervisor suggested that she should discuss this in her therapy and in the meantime she found another client. This one was a woman who had not been able to conceive a child and wanted to talk about the effect of this on her partner and herself. Janet said that she could not work with this because she herself had had an abortion and did not know whether she could conceive in the future. The supervisor lost patience and said, 'Look, if you want to do this work, you will have to face some of the things that you find difficult. Either you see this client or you leave the course.' Janet said that she would see the client. The supervisor was relieved but also anxious that she had pushed the trainee into seeing a client before she was ready.

How can we recognize genuine problems which might prevent a trainee from doing a good enough job and distinguish this from the nerves of a trainee facing the anxiety of seeing a client for the first time? One thing that supervisors need to do is discuss the natural and necessary anxiety of the trainee. Bion said that there should always be two very anxious people in the room. Trainees need to know that a certain level of anxiety before meeting a new client is natural and even necessary. Complacency would be much worse. First sessions can be role-played and examined in detail by a seminar or supervision group before the time comes. *The Trainee Handbook* (Bor and Watts 1999) gives an outline of what to expect in a first session. Although this model would not suit all forms of therapy, it could form the basis of a discussion both of the tripwires that clients may stretch across the path of the unwary and of the kind of boundary issues that need firm but humane handling in a first session. If trainees are reminded that the client is likely to be even more anxious than they are, they may be helped to make more constructive use of their fears, talking to the client about the possible difficulty of beginning with a new person (especially if there has already been one meeting with an assessor).

To return to the problem of placements where trainees are going to be doing the work that might be done by qualified therapists, those who run training courses can contribute to the ethical and professional standards of the counselling or psychotherapy profession by ensuring that the trainees are managed and supervised by qualified therapists. Training courses have much to answer for if they allow trainees to work irresponsibly just because they have to find experience. The course must also take responsibility for the kind of placements that are being used and for the welfare of the clients.

Question 23

Should courses teach classical psychoanalytic viewpoints on, for example, homosexuality and perversion?
Lesley Murdin

Skeletons have a tendency to fall out of cupboards. One basic value shared by all who work in counselling or psychotherapy is a concern for the truth. Unfortunately, there is no one absolute truth in terms of model to be followed, theory or technique. In fact, evidence so far indicates that what works for clients is the relationship with the therapist. This relationship is most effective when the therapist believes in her or his own theory and technique but has not closed her or his mind to other possibilities, in particular to what the client is saying, feeling and doing. That is not to say that any theory or technique will do, but it does indicate a wide variety of possibilities. The first requirement of any training is to ensure that no one does harm. Second, it must seek to equip its trainees to do the best that they possibly can for their clients. Therapists must take the trouble to be as well informed as possible in this and related fields, and this must involve listening to the client's individual needs. Trainees have a right to know about the thinking that has gone on in the past whether or not we now agree with what was said.

These requirements pose dilemmas for the trainer. We cannot deny that sometimes the theorists who have shaped this field have said things that are unacceptable to some people or are just plain wrong. Nothing but harm can come from denying or hiding these problems. For instance, Jung made statements that were uncomfortably racist or pro-Nazi. Freud's ideas about homosexuality have given rise in some of his followers to a view of homosexuality as the result of a failure in development. Some of these ideas are unwelcome but should not be avoided as long as there is plenty of opportunity to put forward and examine a critique.

This particular question is one that might exercise the providers of psychodynamic or psychoanalytic training courses more than any others. Nevertheless, it crystallizes questions about the knowledge base for training for the profession that all trainers need to ask. I shall take two illustrations, one of the issue of racism and the other that of homosexuality. Farhad Dalal published a paper in 1988 claiming that Jung's racism was at the core of his theoretical structure. He argues that Jung's achievement in unifying the human race through his concept of the collective unconscious (Dalal 1988: 263) was achieved at the cost of arguing that we can see the collective unconscious in the so-called primitive tribes that still exist. Jung's argument is that only by a developmental process can we achieve individuality and thinking. Tribes, groups and races have to go through the same sort of developmental processes as individuals and Western European man has achieved the most differentiated, individuated state so far. Reading Jung himself or reading Dalal on Jung, we have to exercise some of the skills of the historian. Jung was a man of his time and any reading of Jung must take account of his context. Charles Rycroft (1988: 281) responded to Dalal by asking whether he had taken account of 'just how current Jung's ethnocentric (sic) arrogant attitude towards savages and primitives was among European intellectuals of his generation'. Otherwise, we are falling into precisely the same errors of judgement ourselves by ignoring the contemporary validity of ways of thinking that may seem alien.

So how is a teacher to deal with this? My suggestion is that a paper like Dalal's could very well be required as set reading for any course that is considering Jung's ideas but that it should be set with the agenda of discovering what there is to be said on the other side. Dalal himself ends his paper with the kind of question that needs to be asked: 'is it possible to rescue the concepts . . . from their racist antecedents?' (Dalal 1988: 278). We are asking students and trainees to make up their own minds and to try to separate useful thinking from the fog of prejudiced argument that has been used to support it.

In the area of sexuality, the problems are different: Freud's original thought is not as homophobic as some of his followers have been in later writing. He emphasizes that human beings are all innately bisexual and that arriving at a heterosexual love is a complex developmental process. It was not until the 1980s that substantial and reasoned critiques of what was seen as the classical viewpoint made their appearance. In 1995 a well-known Kleinian psychoanalyst argued that homosexuals could not be trained to be analysts or therapists because their own developmental deficits meant that they could not be available for the transference relationship in the heterosexual area. In other words, a homosexual therapist could not respond appropriately to the erotic charge directed to the opposite sex parent of the client. This caused immense objection and opposition at the time. Part of the response was a valuable reasoned critique of this view, well summarized by the paper published under the name of Rachel Cunningham, although the writer did feel the need to publish the paper under a pseudonym (1997).

Any training course is liable to come under fire, and rightly so, if it teaches or perpetrates any one view as the truth. Equal opportunities in training mean that anyone has the right to be considered on their own merits for their potential to work constructively within any given model of psychotherapy or counselling. A training course that accepts people without regard to their sexuality or ethnic origin will be likely to foster a debate over theory, and this will undoubtedly enrich the work that can be done with clients. A training course, however, may have to struggle to maintain the right to teach views that are of historical importance and perhaps have some validity when detached from their context.

At the very least, an educated counsellor or therapist needs to have reasons for holding a particular view and this is not possible if the reasons for the contrary views are not studied. Views that are defined as 'oppressive' may not necessarily lack a theoretical rationale, however distasteful or just plain wrong they may be. Teaching the historical development of views on homosexuality should indicate that the picture is very complex. The classical viewpoint on homosexuality is derived from Freud, who wrote that

a person may love:

According to the narcissistic type:

(a) what he himself is,
(b) what he himself was,
(c) what he himself would like to be,
(d) someone who was once part of himself.

According to the anaclitic type:

(a) the woman who feeds him,
(b) the man who protects him.

(Freud 1914: 84)

Freud's account of homosexuality is based on the view that homosexual love and sexuality is essentially narcissistic. As narcissism is a developmental phenomenon that changes as an individual matures, the person who loves only members of the same sex remains, physically and emotionally, in an earlier developmental stage than the heterosexual. According to Freud's theory there could be a progression from this love of oneself or one's own image in another towards the love of someone who is different – of the opposite sex.

Developmental theory here, as in Jung's theory of the development of consciousness, is liable to enshrine value judgements. Development implies progress from point A to point B; from narcissism to love of someone different from oneself; from unselfconsciousness to self-awareness. The more developed position is valued more highly than the less developed position and may be seen as the goal of therapeutic treatment. The only solution to this kind of over-valuation of a norm is to make very clear in training that there are parallel though different developmental paths. Any developmental psychology is bound to be normative but must also be pluralistic. Thus, for example, trainees can be invited to consider what might be a satisfactory homosexual relationship compared with a satisfactory heterosexual relationship. They might be asked to consider whether the same criteria for what is satisfactory might apply to both or whether there are different criteria.

In this as in every aspect of training, trainers must be prepared to reassess their own views and to subject their theoretical teaching to constant scrutiny in the light of what is practical and humane. They must demand evidence that indicates the truth as we can best perceive it at any moment. If teachers can accept being wrong or changing views, they are setting the best possible example of academic integrity to their students.

SECTION 4

Ethics in counselling supervision

Question 24

Is it ethically acceptable for a supervisor with no personal experience of the counselling of couples to supervise those doing that work?
Derek Hill

The question prompts several questions in response:

- What is the competence of the supervisee?
- What is the theoretical orientation of the supervisee?
- How experienced is the supervisor as a caseworker?
- What is the supervisor's training in supervision, and what approach(es) to supervision is/are offered as the basis for a supervision contract?

And to those questions it is of interest to add another:

- Is the intended supervisory relationship mutually desirable or imposed?

Practitioner supervision has different meanings in different contexts. Worldwide, numbers of professional bodies associate supervision with the training phase of professional development. BAC and other counsellor associations assert a requirement for members, in training and trained, to have regular, consistent and appropriate supervision for as long as they undertake casework (BAC 1997: B.6.3.3). For the purposes of this discussion the BAC position is adopted.

Self-evidently, the needs of a trainee, a newly trained and an experienced couple counsellor are different. The trainee requires supervision which is in tune with, and supportive of, the training being received. The newly trained couple counsellor will benefit from supervision which challenges by inviting an exploration of the scope and limits of the competencies already acquired. The 'old hand' may need and want the challenge of supervision informed by radically different perspectives in terms of both theoretical orientation and therapeutic modality.

Couple counsellor trainings based on psychodynamic theoretical frameworks may demand that trainees undergo both personal psychodynamic therapy and the 'apprenticeship' of supervision by a psychodynamically oriented supervisor who is an experienced couple worker. Other forms of training which espouse integrative or eclectic conceptual frameworks may be less restrictive in their prescriptions. In this respect, the ethical quality of a particular supervisory arrangement will depend on the nature of the content of the contract between training institution and trainee.

The supervisor's experience as a caseworker is potentially of significance in two ways from an ethical viewpoint. First, that casework may 'qualify' the supervisor, or not, if experience of couple work is essential. Second, the context in which the casework was undertaken and/or the professional role used to conduct it may or may not provide a sufficient commonality of experience of the application of a specific theoretical approach, of strategic and case-management issues and of ethical dilemmas to permit an appropriate response to a particular supervisee's needs. Here, the ethical quality of a specific supervision contract will depend on the supervisor both declaring their casework experience and using their professional judgement about its relevance to the needs of the supervisee, as well as on the supervisee's own efforts to ensure the fulfilment of their obligations and personal, professional needs.

Although currently in the process of rapid development, the supervision of couple counsellors has existed and been discussed for the better part of fifty years (Skynner 1989). Much of the early practice was informed by psychoanalytic ideas. Langs (1994) offers a fascinating insight into that practice and how it is being adapted to accommodate new understanding about the design of the mind. These forms of supervision are paralleled today by many others, each dedicated to fostering competent practice based on a particular theoretical approach. 'Approach-oriented supervision' (Page and Wosket 1994) places emphasis on the supervisor's mastery of a therapeutic approach and has been vulnerable to the criticism that insufficient attention was given to development of a model of supervision and to development of the skills specific to the role. 'Process-oriented supervision' has been developed in the past decade. Hawkins and Shohet (1989), Page and Wosket (1994) and Holloway and Carroll (1999) each offer a model to serve as the basis for training process-oriented supervision. The growth in eclecticism and in integrative approaches to practitioner training has increased the demand for this form of supervision. Significantly, there is now an expectation that a supervisor will both have expertise as a caseworker and be trained in the skills and disciplines of supervision. As Feltham and Dryden (1994) make clear, a discussion about the relevance of the supervisor's orientation to the role is an essential part of the process of setting up a supervisory contract.

'It seems that whatever approach or method is used, in the end it is the quality of the relationship between supervisor and trainee therapist (or counsellor) that determines whether supervision is effective or not' (Hunt 1986: 20). This quotation turns attention to the way in which supervisor and supervisee are brought together. With so much counselling being undertaken in organizational settings, many practitioners find themselves provided with a supervisor rather than having to search one out. The advantage of the arrangement is that the employer typically takes responsibility for ensuring the competence of the supervisor provided. But that is no guarantee of the quality of the relationship that is established. Supervisors are encouraged to secure consultancy and support for their work (BAC 1995: B.2.3) and that is mandatory in organizations like Relate. The kinds of problem that can arise are described by Martindale *et al.* (1997). But from time to time a situation will arise in which an effective working relationship cannot be sustained. When that occurs the supervisor, the counsellor and the organization all have an ethical responsibility to ensure that different arrangements for supervision are made (BAC 1997: B.6.3).

Conclusion

Setting up an ethically acceptable and effective supervisory relationship is a complicated business. Outside organizations like Relate there are relatively few qualified supervisors who are couple caseworkers, and that increases the problems faced by independent couple counsellors. However, if the issues discussed above are given careful consideration and the nature of a potential contract for supervision is negotiated with frankness on both sides, a wide variety of ethically acceptable arrangements are possible. Casement's (1985) important and appealing concept of the internal supervisor is linked with the atmosphere of the sandpit (playing with different shapes) rather than that of the courtroom (Casement 1990: 13). If the couple counsellor is to acquire the capacity for that playful internal dialogue they will need supervision which is not only ethically acceptable but also inspires, excites and challenges as it engages with the complexities of the primary therapeutic relationship – the adult couple.

Question 25

What is the ethical rationale for having ongoing counselling supervision? BAC obliges members to undertake regular ongoing counselling supervision while my UKCP registration only requires me to be supervised when I need it – which should I follow?
Gabrielle Syme

The Standing Conference for the Advancement of Counselling, who were responsible for the formation of BAC, determined that counselling should be unique in its requirement for regular supervision of all practitioners rather than just for trainees (Jamieson, personal communication). In addition, this supervision should be regular. Thus this requirement featured in BAC's first *Code of Ethics and Practice for Counsellors* (1984: 3.3). Supervision was seen then, as now, as important for monitoring the counselling work. In many respects supervision is the only structured quality control available to the profession.

This decision made counselling unique and was emulated by BPS when it formed a Counselling Psychology Division. UKCP does not mention supervision in its *Ethical Requirements for Member Organisations* (1998), although member organizations of some of its sections do require supervision. An example is the Yorkshire Association of Psychodynamic Psychotherapy, a member of the Psychoanalytic and Psychodynamic Section of UKCP. BAC goes further in specifying in its more recent *Codes of Ethics and Practice for Counsellors* (1990 and

1997) that the volume of supervision 'should reflect the volume of counselling work undertaken and the experience of the counsellor' (B.3.4 and B.6.3.3 respectively). More detail on the criteria to be used in deciding the amount of supervision can be found in another BAC publication, *How Much Supervision Should You Have?* (1998a).

The necessity of supervision for all members of BAC who are counselling naturally led to the production in 1988 of a *Code of Ethics and Practice for the Supervision of Counsellors* and an update in 1995, renamed the *Code of Ethics and Practice for Supervisors of Counsellors*. These outline both the nature of supervision and, through the practice section of the code, good practice for a supervisor.

Apart from making counselling unique, this early decision by BAC has resulted in a lot of thought by practitioners about the benefits to be gained by counsellors from regular supervision, regardless of their seniority and experience. The conviction has grown over the years, although research is needed to verify this, that practice is greatly enhanced by supervision.

In a sense, this conviction of enhanced practice is being wise after the event and the reason for this insistence on supervision at the start may have been related to the role of both the Marriage Guidance Association (now known as Relate) and the Samaritans. Both these associations insisted on their volunteers attending group supervisions or meetings. These meetings offered its members a mixture of group support, a place to off-load feelings and somewhere to explore the relationship with the client(s) and learn from others' experience. All these functions are part of supervision.

Another reason for the insistence on supervision may have been as a safeguard and an acknowledgement that back in 1977 few counsellors had been trained – most had learnt through observing others via an apprentice route – and few counsellors had received counselling, psychotherapy or psychoanalysis to learn about themselves in depth. This contrasted with psychotherapy where even at that time some training took as much as four years and personal therapy was compulsory.

Those who are critical of the necessity of supervision seem to believe that only inexperienced trainees and those who are unanalysed need supervision. It is suggested that a fully analysed practitioner will be sufficiently self-aware not to need supervision to understand their counter-transference in response to projection and transference. I doubt whether anyone who has received good supervision would support this view. Supervision offers more than an analysis of a practitioner's counter-transference.

First, it focuses on the client and thus offers a check on ethical practice and, as mentioned earlier, acts as the quality assurance of the profession. Second, supervision demands honesty and integrity on the part of the counsellor to look critically with another person at the work, identifying the mistakes, doubts and difficulties. However experienced a person is there is more to learn, and supervision offers this so counsellors can monitor their counselling and thus their competence (see Question 7). Third, the parallel process (Searles 1955), in which the dynamics between the counsellor and client are replayed between the counsellor and supervisor, gives an extra window into the client's transference and projections. In addition there is a parallel process from supervisor to supervisee, so that the supportive environment provided by the supervisor is also replayed in the counselling relationship. Fourth, supervision enables the counsellor to unload difficult and distressing information and prevents it being inappropriately unloaded onto family or friends, which would break a core ethical requirement of confidentiality. Last but not least, the client–counsellor relationship is a closed system in which collusion and, even more seriously, sexual, emotional or physical abuse can occur. While supervision cannot prevent this because a devious counsellor can hide it, the experienced supervisor can pick up the unhealthy relationship from the parallel process.

It is for these reasons BAC has an ethical requirement of supervision. The convention between different associations is that the most demanding ethical requirement receives primacy. Thus if other associations do not require supervision but BAC does, anyone who is a member of BAC must have supervision.

Perhaps the most difficult situation is for counsellors whose association does not insist on supervision but advises that it should be had when necessary. How does one assess the need? It is all too easy to be blind to one's own need. Examples follow of some of the feelings and thoughts to look out for and which should act as prompts to seek out supervision. An obvious sign is feeling confused, lost, exceptionally upset or churned up during a session and possibly finding that these feelings do not fade after the session. Another sign is the inability to clear one's head when moving from one client to another. A third sign is a very strong desire to break the contract of confidentiality and talk about a client or a happening in a session to an inappropriate person. Yet another example is the realization that one is treating a particular client differently from all the others.

It is hardest of all when one's association does not insist on supervision. It demands great self-honesty, self-awareness and integrity to seek out supervision without the compulsion of a code of ethics and practice.

Question 26

I have supervised a trained counsellor for the last year and I am not happy with the situation. His work is still poor by my standards but he disputes this. Am I responsible for his mistakes or his future development or work with clients?
Carol Shillito-Clarke

For counsellors and counselling psychologists, supervision is considered an ethical requirement of ongoing practice both during and after training. It is a formal, collaborative relationship in which the counsellor can review and reflect on work with the help of a suitably qualified and experienced colleague who is not so intimately and subjectively involved with the client.

According to the BAC codes, both supervisors and counsellors have an ethical duty to do everything reasonable to ensure the safety of the clients. Supervisors also have a responsibility to promote the safety of the counsellor and to encourage optimum levels of practice and creativity. However, it is the counsellor who holds clinical responsibility for the client (BAC 1995, 1997). In the question posed, the supervisor and counsellor disagree as to whether these responsibilities are being met.

Clinical responsibility and the supervision contract

It may be argued that the relationship between a supervisor and a trained counsellor is a collegial one with each person having respect for the integrity, responsibility and professional judgement of the other. Therefore the extent to which a supervisor may be considered responsible for the mistakes of the counsellor is not easy to define. It may depend, in part, on the nature of the contract or agreement for supervision between the supervisor and the counsellor and, if relevant, the counsellor's employers. It is the supervisor's responsibility to make a contract for the work with each supervisee and to regularly review and renegotiate that contract. Supervision contracts with trainees need to account for additional responsibilities and accountabilities shared with the counsellor's training institution and placement (BAC 1995; Palmer Barnes 1998).

The supervisor has a responsibility to meet her or his contractual and ethical obligations to the counsellor. This includes monitoring and addressing any element of practice that is considered to fall below an ethically acceptable standard. The supervisor would be failing in the duty of care to the counsellor if such practice was overlooked or not challenged, as both counsellor and client could be put at risk. Similarly it is the supervisor's responsibility to ensure that he or she is working within his or her own competence and not giving the counsellor inaccurate or inappropriate advice. Supervisors cannot be held responsible for the counsellor's poor practice if they can demonstrate that they have fulfilled their ethical and contractual obligations to the counsellor.

What does 'poor' mean?

In this question, the first step is to clarify exactly what the supervisor means by 'poor practice'. Is the counsellor incompetent, is his conduct unethical or is his normally competent work impaired in some way? Are the supervisor's standards and expectations inappropriate to the developmental needs of the counsellor (Hawkins and Shohet 1989)? The supervisor needs to clarify in his or her own mind, and then with the counsellor, exactly what is unacceptable and why. The judgement should be supported by appropriate evidence. This is essential in order to address the issue and institute remedial action. It also emphasizes the seriousness of the supervisor's concern and models good practice in respectful investigation. The counsellor can then be clear about the supervisor's perception and what is required of him by way of change (Forrest *et al.* 1999).

Is the counsellor incompetent?

The counsellor in this question is 'trained', which implies that he has been judged competent to practise. However, counselling training programmes vary, as do qualifications, and holding a qualification is not an absolute guarantee of competence to practise. If it can be demonstrated that the counsellor is clearly incompetent to practise, either he has been incorrectly assessed or the standards of the organization that trained him are inappropriately low. In either case it is possible that clients may be put at risk and the public perception of, and faith in, counselling may be damaged. There will also be implications for the counsellor, for his or her employers and for any professional insurance scheme to which they belong.

The supervisor needs to consider, in consultation, the options available for remediation and how the counsellor will be involved. The counsellor will need to receive further help and support to see if he or she can reach an acceptable standard. Such help and support, if accepted, would normally be beyond the remit of supervision, which is not primarily a training relationship (BAC 1995). Addressing the matter with the counsellor's training organization and any employer needs to be handled with respect for the confidentiality of the supervisory relationship.

Is the counsellor working unethically?

At the time of writing, there is no obligation for a counsellor to subscribe to any association or organization with a code of ethics and practice and a complaints procedure. It is for the supervisor to consider if that is a necessary requirement for her or his own contract with counsellors, in line with the BAC recommendations (BAC 1995). Without such a requirement, the supervisor has limited influence to fulfil their ethical duty of care for the client.

If the supervisor believes that the counsellor is working unethically, whether intentionally or not, he or she needs to be clear which clauses of the codes of ethics and practice are being breached, in what way and how often. Supervisors need to be able to impress on counsellors the gravity of any unethical practice, both for themselves and for their clients, and to help them to change and improve. To continue to allow unethical practice by the counsellor could amount to negligence by the supervisor. Making a formal complaint to the counsellor's professional association should be used as a final resort but only after due process of consultation and written warnings.

Is the counsellor's competence impaired?

While there is no agreed definition of 'impairment' in this field, it is generally regarded as implying a level of functioning that is below the person's baseline of adequate competence in one or more areas (Forrest *et al.* 1999). Identifying the nature of the impairment is essential before appropriate remedial action can be taken. Remedial action might include extra supervision, more focused skills work – for example making greater use of tapes, further reading, attendance at specific workshops or courses, or personal therapy.

It may be that the counsellor's competence is impaired by the clinical practice requirements of his employers; for example, the requirement to see a large number of clients in a day without adequate time to maintain suitable records and case-notes. As Carroll (1996b) points out, it can be difficult for a relatively inexperienced counsellor to question their work practice, particularly if they believe that doing so would jeopardize their employment. The role of the supervisor in such circumstances is to support the counsellor in questioning the contract with the employer and negotiating more satisfactory conditions. Where the supervisor has a contract with the counsellor's employers he or she may be able to influence the employer directly, particularly if there is an identifiable risk to the clients. However, in any dealings with the employers, the supervisor must be alert to their duty of confidentiality to the supervisee.

Are the supervisor's standards inappropriate to the counsellor's work?

There is no commonly agreed standard of good practice in counselling. Supervisors' expectations of their supervisees vary widely. This variation in expectations is influenced by supervisors' own drive for perfection, their different training and experience as supervisors, and their different understanding of the requirements of the counsellor's work setting. A further variation may arise out of inherent differences in theoretical orientation, especially in regard to issues such as boundary setting, the nature and degree of active intervention by the counsellor or the form and implementation of the counselling contract. While recognizing such differences, the supervisor does have a responsibility to help the counsellor to develop his or her own skills, expertise and understanding.

Since 1995 all BAC members working as supervisors have been required to review their work regularly with another supervisor or consultant. In addition to self-supervision (Bramley 1996), this is the ideal place to take issues relating to standards and expectations. In such a setting the supervisor's work with, and relationship to, the counsellor may be examined without threatening or compromising the integrity of the work of either.

Does the problem arise out of the interaction between supervisor and counsellor?

It is possible that the supervisor and the counsellor simply do not get on. The reason may be as simple as a clash of personalities, or it may be more complex. Their behaviour towards each other might restimulate memories of past relationships and difficulties with authority (transference and counter-transference). An unacknowledged gender difference may have implications for the power dynamics (Taylor 1994). The failure to get on may reflect some parallel process in which the counsellor lives out, with the supervisor, a difficult relationship with a client or the counsellor's work setting (Hawkins and Shohet 1989, Carroll 1996a). Whatever the reason, the supervisor needs to seek the support and help of their own supervision consultant.

It is appropriate for the supervisor, as the person with the greater authority, to call the counsellor's attention to the poor relationship between them and initiate a discussion. This approach models not only good therapeutic practice but also respect for the counsellor and the 'relationship of referent power and trusting involvement' (Holloway 1995: 107). Within this relationship the counsellor also has an ethical responsibility to raise the issue with the supervisor if client safety is in question (BAC 1997).

What if nothing can be changed?

The preceding paragraphs suggest that the supervisor should take the lead in addressing the relationship with the counsellor. The supervisor needs to be specific about, and offer evidence for, what is perceived to be the 'poor practice' or the difficulty in the relationship, and suggest possible ways forward. If the counsellor continues to reject the supervisor's assessment then one possibility is to invite another senior practitioner, whose experience and orientation are acceptable to both parties, to mediate. If the situation is still not resolvable both parties need to terminate the contract. How this is done is important in terms of each person's professional development and personal learning. Both supervisor and counsellor also need to be clear about what will be said in any reference that the supervisor might be called upon to give in the future. Ultimately the supervisor, unless asked for a reference, has no control over the counsellor's future work with clients even if she or he believes it to be of an inadequate standard or potentially unethical.

Question 27

My supervisee has had to cease counselling very suddenly because of a serious condition. Am I

responsible for the welfare of her clients? Should I take on any of her clients myself if I have space?
Gabrielle Syme

Both the *Code of Ethics and Practice for Supervisors of Counsellors* (1995: B.3.3.11) and the *Code of Ethics and Practice for Counsellors* (1997: B.1.3.9) address the issue of a sudden ending to a counselling relationship. It is the supervisor's duty to discuss with the supervisee the necessity of having arrangements in place to manage a sudden ending and counsellors are instructed that they must have made arrangements for such a happening. The supervisors are also advised that it is good practice for them to be informed of these arrangements. Generally this means that supervisors and counsellors work together to establish a 'disaster plan' with the necessary arrangements for a sudden cessation of counselling.

The 'disaster plan' needs to exist to relieve the counsellor and those closely involved in his or her personal life (spouse, partner, family, friends or colleagues) of a considerable burden in a time of trouble and anxiety. It should identify who is the key person to handle the cessation and inform clients when the counsellor is unable to do so. Obviously those people closely involved with the counsellor need to know of the existence of such a plan, where to find it and how to contact the key person. If this key person is not the supervisor they need to have instructions to inform the supervisor and as to how this contact can be made. This latter provision is necessary because only the supervisor has knowledge of the counsellor's clients since they will have been presented in supervision. The supervisor will know the significant details of clients' life stories, the stage the work has reached and which clients are likely to be particularly vulnerable. Another important reason for contacting supervisors is that as practising counsellors they are well placed to have a discussion with the key person about what to tell clients (this is discussed later). This would be particularly important if the key person is not a counsellor.

The 'disaster plan' also has to have clear instructions on how to access the clients' records and on the systems used by the counsellor to make records secure and to separate clients' names from their addresses and from their case-notes or records so that maximum confidentiality is maintained.

The key person does not have to be a counsellor's supervisor, although their knowledge of the clients is a cogent reason why this may be the best choice. If a supervisor is unwilling to take this role in an emergency then it is wise to choose a counsellor colleague or a lay person who is not likely to be overwhelmed by the sudden crisis because of a close personal involvement and who understands the nature and complexity of counselling work and the vulnerability of some clients. In discussing a 'disaster plan' the supervisor should discuss with the counsellor the suitability of the nominated key person.

One of the major tasks and therefore a major focus of supervision is to address the 'needs of the clients' (BAC 1995: 3.1). This means that the welfare of clients is a prime concern of both the supervisor and supervisee. A natural corollary to this is that counsellors (supervisees) also have a responsibility for the psychological and emotional welfare of their clients. Indeed this is encompassed by the first clause in the section of the *Code of Ethics and Practice for Counsellors* devoted to client safety (1997: B.1.3.1). The responsibility for the welfare of a supervisee's clients is not mentioned specifically in the *Code of Ethics and Practice for Supervisors of Counsellors*; it is implicit. However, in certain counselling settings a supervisor is considered to have some responsibility for a supervisee's clients. Examples would be where a supervisor works for an agency, supervising the work of people counselling in the same agency; or a supervisor working for a counselling training agency and supervising trainees. Overall there is no clear-cut agreement in the profession about whether a supervisor is responsible for the supervisee's clients, nor about the nature of the responsibility (King and Wheeler 1999). Thus a supervisor needs to clarify both when contracting with an agency and with a supervisee.

While there is no clear-cut agreement on a supervisor's responsibility for supervisees' clients, supervisors do become interested and concerned about the welfare of both counsellors and their clients. They are therefore likely to want to assist in whatever ways they can when a counsellor suddenly has such a serious condition that counselling must cease immediately. In addition they have relevant information about counsellors' clients. Thus in practice it is very common for supervisors to agree to be the key person and inform clients should their counsellor be unable to do so.

Before informing any of the clients, probably by telephone, of the sudden cessation of counselling, the supervisor needs to be clear what messages are to be conveyed to the client and think about how to manage the client's shock. It needs to be made clear whether the cessation is expected to be temporary or permanent, and that a client has a right to find another counsellor immediately, although it may be sensible to wait until the situation is clearer. A decision has also to be made about whether clients are told what is actually wrong with the counsellor. This information could invade a counsellor's privacy, would excessively worry certain clients because of identification and will affect future work. On the other hand, some counsellors would consider it a sign of respect for a client to be given as much accurate and honest information as is possible.

A further issue to be considered before informing clients is what support can be offered them to assist in managing the sudden cessation and, if it is permanent, transferring to a new counsellor. Possibilities are further brief telephone calls with a clear understanding of who is initiating these calls; face-to-face counselling session(s) or telephone counselling session(s) (the financial basis of both these offers needs to be clear); suggestions of other counsellors that could be approached; suggestions of how to find the names of other counsellors in the area (such as BAC's *UK Counselling and Psychotherapy Directory 2000*, UKCP's *National Register of Psychotherapists*, BCP's *2000 Register of Psychotherapists* or BPS's *Directory of Chartered Psychologists*); and an attempt to help clients identify other support available to them. What is offered will depend on whether the cessation is permanent or temporary, the availability of the supervisor both in terms of time and personal resources and the client's personal financial situation, emotional state and response to the bad news.

Supervisors are under no obligation to see their supervisees' clients in the case of a sudden cessation and may not have the time to do so. If they do, they are unlikely to take on more than one or two. If a supervisor does have the time to take on more clients it would be unwise to make the decision without talking it through with their own supervisor or with an experienced colleague. It is important to think through the possible consequences for the client first and foremost, but also for the counsellor should he or she be able to return to work with that client, any future counsellor and oneself.

If the cessation is permanent the client is likely to need therapeutic help to come to terms with the sudden break which is effectively a 'death'. Assuming the supervisor has no vacancies then the client may need temporary support, preferably from the supervisor, if at all possible, while the move to another counsellor is made. Making telephone contact available at agreed times and on agreed terms will probably be sufficient. Face-to-face counselling sessions would build in complications for a future counsellor, so the perceived need of the client for this type of support needs to be weighed against the impact on the client of the involvement of another counsellor. This can simply add to the chaos and create greater problems in any future counselling relationship.

If a supervisor does decide to offer counselling to his supervisee's client, there is bound to be work on loss. In addition it is possible that there could be idealization or vilification of the 'lost' counsellor with the new counsellor being cast in the opposite mould. Should the life story of the client include sudden loss, particularly of a parent, this material is likely to feature in the work. Clients are bound to wonder about a counsellor before meeting them and are likely also to have some fantasies about them as well. The fantasies may be rather different when a supervisor becomes the counsellor because the client will have known of the existence of a supervisor, possibly known their name and found out something about them. In addition, the supervisor might be imagined as a grandparent. If this is the case then this could be part of the transference relationship set up in the counselling relationship with the 'lost' counsellor's supervisor. It is important to discover in the first session what facts and fantasies the client holds.

If the cessation is temporary, supervisors are again under no obligation to see their supervisees' clients, but may want to be helpful and offer telephone support to 'hold' the client until the counsellor resumes work. It may be unwise to offer face-to-face counselling because of the effect this will have on both the counselling and the supervisory relationships when the counsellor (supervisee) returns. Some of the possible effects on the counselling relationship have been discussed and particularly where the break is short (six to eight weeks) would simply complicate the relationship unnecessarily. It will be hard enough for the returning counsellor and the break itself will bring enough work in its own right without further complications. The effects on the supervisory relationship could be to stimulate competition and even hate and envy between the supervisor and supervisee. This would be particularly so if the supervisor is seen as all good and the counsellor on returning to work becomes the recipient of a strong negative transference. One would need to guard against this type of interaction.

Of course there comes a point when it would be clear that neither to offer therapy nor to enable the client to work temporarily with, or move permanently to, another counsellor would be unnecessarily harsh. This would have to be assessed sensitively and sympathetically. Clearly this is another area where consultation with one's own supervisor would be wise so there is someone with whom to think through the various options and the needs of the supervisee, the client and oneself before taking any action.

It is important that the supervisor attends to their own needs as well. It does not help anyone if the supervisor takes on too much work through a mistaken sense of duty or need to rescue the supervisee or client and then collapses, letting down many more people. Counselling and supervision are not about creating a perfect world or preventing difficult times, but about facing the reality that life at times can be very difficult and people need to discover the resources to manage. Rescuing people might not allow these resources to be discovered.

SECTION 5

Ethics in research

Question 28

How do counsellors and clients measure an effective counselling relationship? What precautions are necessary in follow-up evaluation of counselling? What are the implications for the counsellor and the profession?
Caroline Jones

Before looking at how counsellors and clients measure an effective counselling relationship, the question 'why' requires brief attention:

- to determine whether the client has achieved their therapeutic aims and goals within a reasonable timescale,
- for the sake of professionalism (Howard 1998) and reflective practice (McMahon 1999), as counselling cannot be classified as a profession unless there is a body of evidence to justify process and outcomes,
- to establish the relative effectiveness of theoretical approaches for particular problems and individual clients,
- to obtain and justify resources for agencies and within institutions,
- to manage resources effectively,
- for the sake of counsellor 'job satisfaction', and
- to identify individual training and continuing professional development (CPD) needs.

It is more complex to determine how as this inevitably involves some subjectivity by both counsellors and clients about a process that is as much an art and craft as a science. This question discusses some of the ethical and practical issues involved, for the counsellors and clients together and separately both during and after their counselling relationship.

Measuring effective counselling involves the tasks of monitoring and evaluation, defined as follows.

> 'Monitoring' refers to the gathering, whether on a regular or occasional basis, of basic statistical information about counselling activity.
>
> Examples of monitoring might include: the number of clients seen in a year; their gender and ages; sources of referral.
>
> 'Evaluation' refers to the making of informed judgements (including comparative judgements) about the effectiveness of particular counselling practice.
>
> (BAC 1996a)

Central to the provision of ethical counselling are the requirements of doing most good and causing least harm. Clients should be informed in pre-counselling information of any monitoring and evaluation that the counsellor routinely undertakes and counsellors should be ready to justify collecting data that comes under the terms of the Data Protection Act 1998. During counselling, counsellors need to find their own ways of ensuring that clients can express any dissatisfaction or concerns as these occur. This is achieved by holding periodic reviews or by offering other opportunities for assessment and depends on the counsellor's style, theoretical approach and philosophy. My own client evaluation form is based on learning from others (Sutton 1987; BAC Research Committee 1989), and attempts to offer something of benefit to my clients as well as to myself. It comprises four questions:

1 What was my motivation for coming to counselling?
2 Were the goals I defined appropriate/realistic for me?
3 How did the counselling process help me?
4 How will the experience of counselling help me to deal with any future difficulties I may encounter?

All clients are given this form at the first session and encouraged to use it only if and when they so wish and to send comments to me, anonymously. The proportion of forms returned is not representative so this method of measuring effectiveness can be only one of several.

Effectiveness of counselling normally includes an assessment of progress by the client towards their initial and subsequent goals. This avoids the dangers identified by Ellis (1997) and Watchell (1997a) of sustaining apparently valued counselling relationships without these necessarily contributing to any progress towards the goals of counselling. Goals can be wide ranging and general or more focused, according to the client's purpose in seeking counselling. A particularly useful question, 'how will you know when things are getting better?', helps the client to identify and look out for progress. Scaling questions also measure progress and are a helpful way to establish when to end. The counsellor's expectations may differ from the client's about the timing of the ending (O'Connell 1998).

A more general method of monitoring effectiveness after the counselling relationship involves regular audits of endings and analysing these against other data. Relevant data varies according to setting: waiting times for first session, overall number of sessions, frequency of sessions, presenting and underlying problems, gender, ethnic origin, age, disability (where known) and sexual preference (where known). Such information assists the individual counsellor in determining whether any one of these factors influences effectiveness, so that further training needs and other management issues can be identified. An example of a management issue is the responsibility in funded settings to demonstrate that the counselling provision is meeting the needs of the client population in an equitable way. This includes not only the take-up of the service but the outcomes. This more statistical kind of monitoring need not be beyond the capabilities of any counsellor (Sanders and Liptrot 1993).

All the routes to measuring effectiveness can be explored and analysed in counselling supervision as these may point to the need to adapt and change practice. Openness to change is a strength for any counsellor and a powerful model for clients.

Precautions needed in follow-up evaluation of counselling include

- reference to the possibility of this in pre-counselling literature,
- written express consent by the client when contracting,
- discussion with the client about the methods used and any issues of confidentiality such as the effect of receiving written communications at home marked 'confidential',
- renewing consent at regular intervals during the period of evaluation so that unwanted intrusions at a later date are avoided, and
- clarity about the aims of the research, who is conducting this and if and where findings will be published if this is planned.

The profession has a responsibility to ensure that all clients receive quality help. Individually, counsellors can develop an awareness of those counselling relationships where there is a reasonable expectation that the way they work (their approaches and philosophy) benefits clients. Clients who require a different approach can be referred on; discussing this with clients can be therapeutically helpful in itself. Although conducting research is not an ethical requirement for individual counsellors who are members of BAC, it is an ethical requirement to be able to recognize those occasions when it is appropriate to refer clients elsewhere (BAC 1997: B.6.1.4). By having a good knowledge of counselling provision and other appropriate resources locally, the approaches used and the relative strengths and weaknesses of these for particular problems, counsellors can make good referrals and therefore assist clients in meeting their needs.

In conclusion, the profession has several responsibilities in regard to measuring the effectiveness of counselling. Counsellors individually need to check whether they are helping clients and how this is achieved. An additional benefit for many counsellors is the contribution that sound research makes towards justifying the necessary resources to fund agency and institutional provision of counselling services, thereby increasing the availability of counselling to those who seek this form of help. Equally important is that research underpins public confidence in counselling more generally.

Question 29

How does the profession of counselling manage the demand for evidence-based research that counselling is effective when this poses risks to clients particularly in the context of services delivered in an agency or institutional setting?
Derek Hill

One of the challenges still facing the counselling profession is the task of finding a way to communicate to the public, and to potential clients, exactly what counselling offers them. Numbers of attempts have been made and one of these is to be found as one of the introductory paragraphs to BAC's *Code of Ethics and Practice for Counsellors* (1997). This speaks about the qualities of counselling but it doesn't offer much help if the 'cost-benefits' of counselling are questioned. 'The counsellor's role is to facilitate the client's work' (BAC 1997). That suggests what we, as practitioners, know – that the outcomes of counselling depend both on the ability of clients, helped by the counsellor, to identify realistic purposes, and on the counsellor's abilities to tap the clients' motivations and resources so that those purposes can be achieved. But we also know that these are not linear processes, that external influences are at work, that motivations modify and that purposes may need to change. Counselling is at best a brief intervention in clients' lives and one of the ethical issues faced is when it should be terminated. When is it better for the clients that counselling is no longer a direct influence on their lives? Given the uniqueness of each client and of the constellation of internal and external influences on their lives, it is not easy to contrive forms of research which will answer the potential client's question about the benefits counselling will offer them, and about its personal and monetary costs. It is certainly easier to provide evidence for those who fund counselling services that a particular kind of improvement in well-being is achieved in a stated proportion of an identified category of client, and to make cost comparisons with chemotherapy, for example.

So 'evidence-based research that counselling is effective' is itself a highly problematic enterprise. It would be false to assume that the uses made of any such research findings would themselves be 'scientific'. The circumstances and prejudices of potential clients, and the politics of funding public services, result in research findings being treated to a greater or lesser extent as marketing messages. If a moment's consideration is given to the processes by which 'purchasing decisions' are made by individuals and public bodies about medicines, on which there is typically a wealth of 'objective' information, the use of research in the sometimes less than totally ethical business of marketing will be understood. These thoughts prompt the question of whether research to demonstrate the efficacy of counselling is ethically justifiable.

Having sounded that note of caution, the risks associated with research into counselling need consideration. Setting the researcher on one side, there are potentially five individuals or bodies which may be exposed to risk: the client, the counsellor, the supervisor, the organization or institution providing the counselling and the professional body. There is also the risk that the integrity of the counselling process will be compromised and thus its potential benefits diminished. Viewed from an ethical standpoint, the people and bodies concerned are all capable of negotiating with the researcher the nature of their involvement, the safeguards against identified risks and the uses to which research findings will be put. That fact enables ethical research to be designed and carried out.

The association of research procedures with the process of counselling creates changes in it; some of these can be foreseen and regulated, and some cannot be known until both counselling and research activities are concluded. The changes in process which can be foreseen will be those that are the focus of negotiation with the parties involved. The unpredictable changes may either increase or diminish the perceived benefits of counselling. For example, it was found in a Relate-based study that the involvement of clients in the completion of a questionnaire after every counselling session had the effect of making them and their counselling feel special and more valuable (Shapiro and Barkham 1993).

'Positive' consequences such as that described, and other 'negative' effects, can be evidenced by the use of statistical techniques but that does not remove the ethical issue related to the compromising of the counselling process. It is not possible to know the precise differences between the outcomes of the researched and unresearched counselling of a particular client since the process will have taken place in one or other context. It might appear that this argument is only of significance to researchers and that in practical terms it is a matter of the best being enemy of the good. It none the less presents counselling with an ethical dilemma because the nature and extent of the impact of a research involvement on the outcomes of counselling is a) uncertain, b) a consequence of a procedure which is not an integral part of the counselling process and c) more often than not a diversion from achievement of the client's immediate purposes. Specifically, such research involvements introduce an unnecessary and imponderable influence into the counselling. That dilemma is commonly dealt with by offering assurances, which may be more or less well grounded in verifiable findings, that no serious disadvantage will be experienced by the client if involvement in research is agreed. In the physical sciences it is well understood that the features of a system cannot be measured without changing the system itself. The complexity of the 'counselling system' is such as to make it ethically questionable whether statistically based assurances should be offered. Perhaps a direct appeal to the altruism of the client would be a more appropriate response to the dilemma.

Bollas and Sundelson (1995) raise a separate issue. The 'betrayal of confidentiality', which is to some degree a feature of any research into counselling, is argued to be eroding the confidence of clients to the point at which the counselling process itself breaks down. This is an issue for the profession. Collectively, counsellors, psychotherapists and analysts have it in their power to protect the integrity of the confidence-based, private processes they offer to the public by resisting the demands of managed care, the other professions to which clients may be referred, researchers and the courts. It might be argued that one research project more or less is not going to bring about the downfall of psychotherapeutic practice, but there is no central, controlling body and it therefore falls to all practitioners to attend to this threat and to consider most carefully the ways in which the ethical dilemmas associated with research are 'dealt with'. The term 'dealt with' is used deliberately here because the issues being discussed are very good examples of those which 'no code can resolve' and concerning which 'members must determine which parts [in the code] apply to particular settings, taking account of conflicting responsibilities' (BAC 1997: 2.2).

The amount of research into counselling grows year by year, not least because growing numbers of counsellors are working for Master's degrees and find themselves obliged by university regulations to engage in research activity. Another cause for that growth is the need for the providers of counselling to secure public and private funds. The conflict of interest in these situations has to do both with the survival of counselling organizations and their services and with the immediate well-being of the clients. The research activities of agencies and institutions turn our attention to the question of whether the clients of those bodies are particularly at risk. It is suggested that some of the best and most carefully designed research, and some of the most exploitative studies, have been undertaken by organizations responsible for counselling services. Equally, both excellent and highly unethical research work has been done with the clients of the independent sector. If there is an argument in favour of organizationally based research it is that those managed environments have the potential to implement the complex research projects which derive a maximum of data from well-characterized and carefully protected client groups. It is those bodies which also have the potential to set the standards for research and to ensure that the downfall of psychotherapeutic services does not result from the 'betrayal of confidentiality' referred to earlier. BAC took a very important step in that direction when it published its Information Guide 4, *Ethical Guidelines for Monitoring, Evaluation and Research in Counselling* (1996, reprinted 1997) the content of which is commended to the reader.

SECTION 6

Other important questions

Question 30

What are the arguments for and against avoidable dual relationships or multiple relationships such as being a counsellor and a trainer, a trainer and a supervisor or a supervisor to a work colleague who is also a friend?
Carol Shillito-Clarke

A dual or multiple relationship is one in which one person has more than one role or relationship in respect to another person. Each may be purely professional or a combination of professional and personal relationships, they may also be sequential or concurrent. Examples would include making a close friendship with a trainee or client during or immediately after the professional contact, supervising a counsellor to whom you are also the trainer or line-manager, or counselling a therapist whose manager is currently your supervisee.

All codes of ethics consider it unethical to combine a sexual relationship with a professional role. Many professional codes of ethics also preclude the practitioner having a personal as well as professional relationship with a client. The key ethical principles here are those of respecting the autonomy of the person who holds less power and authority (such as the client, supervisee or trainee) and ensuring that they remain a partner in a just and trustworthy professional relationship (the professional relationship always takes precedence over any personal relationship). Some, such as BAC and the BPS Division of Counselling Psychology, specifically preclude certain professional dual relationships such as practitioners having a second role as a tutor or supervisor with their clients (BAC 1995 and 1997; BPS DCoP 1998).

The main problem with dual or multiple relationships with another person is that the two or more roles may not be mutually supportive or compatible. Where the boundaries implicit in the different roles meet or overlap, they may become blurred or eroded and weakened. The rules negotiated for one relationship may interfere with those negotiated for the other relationships. Conflicts of interest may be hard to avoid, responsibilities may become confused, objectivity may be reduced and professional judgement may be compromised, particularly where one person holds more power than the other. These processes may be hard to hold in awareness and monitor consciously. Those who hold a psychodynamic orientation also see a dual relationship as compounding the transference. At worst, a dual relationship may promote the conditions for an abuse of power and exploitation (Rutter 1990; Russell 1993).

It is important to remember that while most therapeutic and supervision relationships are conducted on a one-to-one basis, the participants are also members of wider professional and social communities. Where the two people involved in a dual relationship are also working closely with others, such as with a training or supervision group, or as practitioners in the same organization, their relationship will affect the broader group dynamic. The more personal and intense the dual relationship, the more potential there will be for further effects in the wider group.

Another problem associated with dual or multiple relationships is the maintenance of confidentiality. The blurring of significant boundaries is more likely when people meet frequently in different roles as often happens, for example, in counsellor training. Some training organizations offer trainees supervision and personal development groups with one of their own members. The BAC *Code of Ethics and Practice for Trainers* is clear that 'the providers of counselling for trainees during the programme must be independent of the training context and any assessment procedures' (BAC 1996b: B.1.6.2). The compromise, which is sometimes reached, is that a trainer on the course may supervise a student's work or lead a personal development group, as long as they do not take the role of a personal tutor. In such circumstances, it is important to avoid judgements about a student's professional ability being confounded by knowledge of their personal circumstances. It can be difficult to ensure that knowledge and confidential information gained by one person is kept from others particularly if the training team is a small one.

Dual and multiple relationships are not always avoidable or perceived as undesirable by other professionals and there may be considerable pressure on practitioners to 'double up' on their work roles. The pressures may be contextual, theoretical, organizational or personal and may lead to further ethical dilemmas. For example, compromises are justified in order to keep the cost of training or therapy to a minimum so as not to discriminate financially against the client or trainee.

Avoiding a dual relationship is easier when there is a wide choice of practitioners. For instance, there is more likely to be a choice of practitioners to act as therapists and supervisors in urban areas than in less densely populated areas. Lack of choice can also be a problem for students if their training institution specializes in a particular discipline or theoretical approach. Similarly, choice is restricted if only senior practitioners are considered appropriate as supervisors or therapists in order to preserve the rigour or 'theoretical purity' of the learning experience.

Professional services and organizations such as social services, psychology services, employee assistance programmes and agencies do not all share the same sensitivity to the issues of professional dual relationships. Such organizations also have justifiable concerns about quality assurance and the cost-effectiveness of their counselling services. This can become a significant source of ethical difficulty for the counsellors, especially if they are asked to work with other employees (Carroll 1996b). The question becomes 'who is my client and therefore to whom am I responsible for holding confidentiality and other such boundaries?'. All counsellors who are members of BAC, or whose employing organization is a BAC member, are required to have access to an independent consultant on a regular basis if they are supervised by their line-manager (BAC 1997).

Practitioners can also experience considerable intrapersonal pressure to take up a dual role. Resisting an invitation to work with a friend or colleague whom one likes, feels sorry for or admires can be difficult. Feeling flattered, doing someone a favour, having the chance to increase one's income or influence or to become part of a new development may all be persuasive arguments for adopting a dual role against one's better judgement. It should be remembered, however, that even the most professional people are not infallible and that the best-regulated relationships can be subject to unexpected stresses leading to damaging mistakes.

Some professionals consider that imposing restrictions on dual roles are reflective of an outdated Western, analytical approach to therapy that is primarily concerned with protecting the transference and is no longer relevant. Wosket (1999) quoting Hedges *et al.* (1997) suggests that arguments for allowing dual relations include

- greater creativity and potential benefits for the therapy especially in terms of creating a 'real' relationship,
- creating a situation more reflective of the changing nature of inter-personal boundaries and the reality of people living in the same community,
- having a greater multicultural relevance and recognition of what may constitute appropriate relationship boundaries in a particular community and
- recognizing that it is not the dual relationship that is a problem but its abuse by unethical and incompetent practitioners.

Wherever one is sympathetic or antagonistic to the idea of dual or multiple roles, there is need for careful consideration and consultation before entering into such relationships. Pearson and Piazza (1997) suggest that because most dual and multiple relationships tend to emerge and develop rather than happen suddenly they can be anticipated and managed. Examples of those that arise out of professional work requirements or as a result of structural changes or the development of one role into another have been mentioned above. In addition, there are those that are coincidental, such as meeting a client at the supermarket or concert, or are deliberately created by the 'predatory professional' with the aim of seducing or exploiting the client. These may be harder to avoid but still need to be managed and, in the case of the latter, brought to an end.

All the parties involved in dual and multiple relationships need to question alternative solutions and discuss the position independently with other senior practitioners of differing opinions. Where other people are closely involved, for example group members or members of the training or counselling team, their opinion should also be sought.

The following points need to be addressed:

- the nature of the proposed relationship, whether it is sequential or concurrent,
- the issue of any power differential and the length and nature of the pre-existing relationship,
- in the case of a previous counselling relationship, the focus and feature of the client's work, their degree of vulnerability, and the way in which the contract was or is to be ended,
- how each person perceives the respective roles, the boundaries and

possible role conflicts both when they start the relationship and in the future,

- that the responsibility for the relationship and for any consequences will be held by the person with the greater authority; for example, a supervisor must be prepared to override a friendship and make a complaint against a friend or supervisee in order to protect a client from unethical practice and
- how each party will monitor their experience of the relationship and maintain the boundaries of the relationship against slippage or erosion.

Dual and multiple relationships occur frequently in daily life. In the world of counselling, supervision and training they are not always avoidable and may not be harmful. It is not always possible to predict whether more than one relationship can safely be held because it is not always obvious at the outset how circumstances may change. What is certain is that in every case, all parties involved need to be aware of and clear about the implications for practice. To this end it is important that the issue of dual and multiple relationships is addressed and debated both in training and throughout the practitioner's working life. 'Confusion in core relationships invariably results in confusion in the candidate. Candidates who experience such confusion often fail to question it and replicate this confusion in their own work' (Palmer Barnes 1998).

Question 31

How should an employing agency or institution support counsellors and manage the occasions when a client refuses to work with a counsellor at first sight, due to race, culture or disability or for other reasons?
Roger Casemore

We work in a profession which believes implicitly in the principle of valuing difference in other people, no matter what that difference may be, affirming both the common humanity and uniqueness of each individual (BAC 1997: B.2.1) and ensuring that an anti-discriminatory approach is integral to our practice (BAC 1997: A.2).

Among our responsibilities as counsellors we have a primary ethical duty to respect the autonomy of the client (BAC 1997: B.1.5.1), which includes their right to enter into counselling and to do this with a counsellor of their choice. This must include the client having the right to choose not to work with a counsellor, for whatever reason they choose and in fact not to give any reason for rejecting a counsellor.

Sadly, in our society today, the social stereotype of a counsellor is still predominantly that of a white, middle-aged, middle-class female. While we know within the profession that there is a much greater human variety in counsellors than that stereotype expresses, potential clients may have very different expectations of what their counsellor may be like, based on their prejudices and on the stereotypes of which they are aware, both of which may have formed the basis on which they may have chosen to go into counselling. Some clients may have specifically asked to see either a counsellor who is very similar to them in their differences or one who is very different. I have had experience of clients from one minority ethnic background very clearly not wanting a counsellor from within their own ethnic community and having good reasons, in their own mind, for that choice. Some clients may have expectations of what their counsellor will be like, on the basis of the agency for which the counsellor works or the geographical or social setting in which their private practice is located. Other clients may be strongly prejudiced against individuals or social groups who are different in some way and that prejudice may be so strong that they are unable to trust or relate to an individual counsellor who is different in that way. In any of these situations clients could be quite surprised to find their counsellor is very different to what they were expecting and could even therefore experience shock, disappointment, fear or anger and react accordingly.

One strategy which counselling organizations could use to reduce the likelihood of such incidents occurring would be to make some changes in the publicity they use for their services. To some extent the language of counselling and the ways in which counselling services are marketed do little to make it clear and explicit that difference is valued in counsellors and clients and in counselling. The language of counselling can itself be discriminatory and can reinforce the stereotype of a middle-class service for middle-class, white people. Developing different marketing approaches and publicity materials which are designed to promote ease of access for all sectors of the community could do much to counteract the stereotyping of counsellors and counselling and some misunderstandings about the nature of the service being offered would be less likely to occur.

When clients treat us differently and discriminate against us on grounds of difference, that can be a painful and even shocking experience. Ideally, a counsellor would be emotionally healthy and resourceful enough to cope with what might be perceived as at least a professional slight or at most hurtful personal discrimination and rejection. However, a counsellor who is rejected by a client on any of the grounds cited in the question might feel very hurt, angry and devalued through being rejected in this way. A counsellor who, for whatever reason, is in some way vulnerable at the time of the event, or is perhaps less experienced, may find it less easy to manage and contain those feelings and could be seriously affected.

All counsellors in membership of BAC are bound by the code (BAC 1997) B.6.1 (competence) and B.6.2 (counsellor safety). Those of us working in private practice have to take full responsibility for our own self-management and for monitoring and maintaining our own emotional health. Good and regular supervision and personal therapy enable us to maintain our emotional health and our objectivity about the job we do as counsellors. Counsellors working in agencies have no less a duty of care for themselves, particularly if they have individually signed to abide by the codes of ethics and practice. However, they can and should expect their employers to take some responsibility for that as well.

Organizations and agencies which take out membership of BAC sign to say that, as an organization, they will abide by the codes and that they will ensure that counsellors working for them also abide by the codes. In some agencies individual counsellors do not take out individual membership of BAC if the agency has taken out organizational membership, while in others they do. Employers have a responsibility under employment law to carry out a duty of care towards their employees and this includes counsellors. In recent years there has been legislation, backed up by case law, in relation to the necessity for employers to provide appropriate care for the physical and the emotional health of their employees. The Institute of Personnel and Development (0208 263 3355) publishes a number of information sheets on good practice in the employment of staff along with guidance, advice and information on supporting staff in stressful occupations (and counselling is indeed stressful).

Good practice in the employment of counsellors suggests that employers should ensure that counsellors are effectively managed through the provision of good managerial supervision and appraisal along with the provision of effective monitoring and support of their counselling by appropriate levels of supervision and opportunities for continuing professional development. This should include the opportunity to have their supervision paid for and to be able to take it during working hours. I would suggest also they should have the opportunity to have personal therapy related to their ongoing professional development (for example to meet the criteria for accreditation) during working hours as well, and perhaps even to have that paid for.

I recognize that some employers might consider this latter point as something that employees should do in their own time, particularly as much of personal therapy will be about their personal rather than professional development. However, as counsellors applying for accreditation are now required to have undertaken a minimum of 40 hours of personal therapy or its equivalent it seems to me that this is a requirement that employers should enable their employees to meet.

While there are an increasing number of counselling agencies employing and paying counsellors, there are a continuing number of agencies which are voluntary or charitable organizations using volunteer counsellors. In most of these organizations volunteer counsellors should be regarded and treated as employees who are covered by employment law. There is as much a duty of care for organizations in employing volunteers as there is in employing paid staff. Therefore volunteer counsellors have as much right as paid counsellors to be carefully and sensitively managed, and to be provided with good line-management supervision and appraisal along with effective counselling supervision and opportunities for continuing professional development.

If a client chooses not to work with a counsellor on grounds of difference, this is clearly an agency management issue as well as an issue for the particular counsellor concerned. There needs to be open discussion between the management, counsellors and supervisors about the possibility of such an event happening. This discussion needs to lead to agreement on what the agency reaction will be, first of all to the potential client and second, but equally, to the counsellor concerned. While protecting the confidentiality rights of the potential client, the agency needs to determine if and how the counsellor is to be told such an event has occurred and how the agency has responded. If the counsellor is informed, they should have the opportunity to discuss this with their line-manager and also be able to take it to supervision as soon as possible, so that they can explore their reactions. The counsellor will also need to know to whom they can talk about the incident within the organization, such as the other counsellors, or if the matter is just to be kept between them and their line-manager. It may be that knowledge of the incident could prejudice another counsellor working with that client, or it could be helpful. There may be a strong case for discussing such incidents openly in meetings or case discussion groups so that feelings can be articulated and contained and all clients can continue to be offered an effective service.

The reaction to the client will also call for some sensitivity. I have always felt that most clients are extremely anxious about going for counselling and that for many it takes a very great deal of effort to pluck up the courage to go that very first time. Having done that it must take even more courage to be able to reject a counsellor that the client does not feel is right for them, whatever the reasons. The agency will need to enable the client to feel heard and understood and be able to offer the client ways of finding a counsellor who will be acceptable for them.

However, if the client's choice is clearly influenced by excessive and inappropriate prejudice, this may prove very difficult for the agency to deal with. While no one who needs help should be turned away, at the same time agencies and counsellors must be able to make decisions about who they are able to work with and who they are unable to help and need to reject or to refer elsewhere. The agency needs to have discussed and agreed with counsellors the grounds for rejection or referral, the ways in which the agency will react in such a situation and how such a referral or rejection would be managed.

As counsellors working with the vulnerabilities of others we open up our own vulnerabilities and take the risk of being hurt by those we seek to serve. We do not need to accept being left alone to deal with our pain if the actions of our clients leave us feeling hurt or rejected. That will surely leave us less able to help the next and subsequent clients who come to us. It is our primary responsibility to take care of ourselves and to ensure that we are fit and capable to do our work. For those who are employed, their employers have an equal duty to protect and care for their staff and to ensure that they have adequate resources to support them in the job they are doing, whether in a paid or in a voluntary capacity. There is also an organizational responsibility to protect counsellors, as well as their clients, from avoidable harm. Promoting appropriate and relevant images of their service and the people who deliver it could do much to help.

Question 32

Sex or sexual activity with a client, trainee or supervisee is unethical in our profession but what constitutes sexual activity in a counselling, training or supervisory relationship?
Carol Shillito-Clarke

The reason that 'sexual activity' is hard to define is that it is a social construct: a set of behaviours and attributes that a group of people have agreed to classify and label. Any social construct is open to varying interpretation, depending on the perceptions and beliefs of the particular culture, group or individual responsible for the classification. Such perceptions and beliefs also change with time and circumstance. A powerful example would be the way homosexuality has been defined and redefined over the last 50 years, first to include then to exclude sexual deviation and mental disorder (Kutchins and Kirk 1997).

Sexual activity may be deemed to include anything from sexual intercourse to hugging, kissing or touching; from sexualized language or interpretation of therapeutic material to the way one person questions another about their personal relationships; from suggesting that clothing be undone or removed to standing too close to another person. In any interaction between two people, each person's emotional and physical experience, together with their perception of the context, and the nature of, and intention behind, the other's behaviour will contribute to the construct.

Because there is no single definition of sexual activity, the boundaries of what constitutes ethically acceptable behaviour in the therapeutic, supervisory or training setting will be different between individuals, therapeutic schools, organizations and cultures. For instance, within the *Code of Ethics* for the British Association for Sexual and Relationship Therapy (BASRT 1996, reviewed in 1999), it is considered acceptable for a specialist sex therapist to discuss in detail the most intimate aspects of a client's sex life. An invitation to such sexual intimacy would be considered ethically inappropriate for a general counsellor. Psychodynamic practitioners may avoid all forms of body contact with their clients, a practice that many Humanistic therapists may see as therapeutically important. Although both Jung and Perls had affairs with their clients (Masson 1992), all the major codes of ethics and practice now consider a sexual relationship with a client to be gross malpractice.

Before trying to address the question of where the ethical boundaries around sexual activity in therapy, supervision and training may lie, it is necessary to recognize that issues of sexuality extend beyond the content of the work. It can be argued that because all humans are sexual beings, sexual energy, active or latent, conscious or unconscious, will be present in all interactions. This is not to suggest that all therapeutic work is essentially about sex or needs to be interpreted as such. It is recognition that issues of sexuality are important, particularly in the emotionally intense interactions often generated within the therapeutic process. It is the responsibility of the practitioner (therapist, supervisor or trainer) to be alert to, and to be able to work with, that process ethically. It is also their responsibility to recognize that the other (client, supervisee or trainee) may perceive the process very differently. A common experience cannot be assumed even between people of the same sex. For example, a woman therapist might make a gesture of comfort towards her female client who misperceives it as having a sexual intention.

Bond (1993) suggests that there are three categories of sexual activity of ethical concern to the therapeutic relationship: sexual assault, sexual abuse and sexual harassment. All three are forms of exploitation, which provide self-gratification for the more powerful person and are without regard for the autonomy and beneficence of the other. The consequences of such exploitation for the client are usually highly damaging (Russell 1993). All forms of sexual exploitation are prohibited by the codes of ethics of all major organizations (BAC 1997; BPS 1998; UKCP 1998).

Some codes of ethics such as those of BAC and the BPS Division of Counselling Psychology (DCoP) also consider sexual exploitation of students by trainers unethical. Although it may be argued that the relationship is very different from that of counsellor–client and the material shared is less intimate, the student may be just as emotionally vulnerable to the perceived power and charisma of the trainer. The student may also feel professionally vulnerable if they are dependent on the trainer for a favourable evaluation in order to qualify. Even if the trainer is not directly responsible for the student's evaluation, other staff members and students may feel compromised by the relationship, however 'secret', and the student be unfairly persecuted. Here, as elsewhere, the trainer has a responsibility to model ethical behaviour, appropriate management of boundaries and recognition of ethical dilemmas (Webb 1997).

Both BAC and the Division of Counselling Psychology also consider sexual relationships between supervisors and supervisees unethical, even if the relationship is between two people who are professional peers and might otherwise be considered 'consenting adults'.

However personally 'equal', the supervisor still holds a professional responsibility for the supervisee and such an emotionally charged dual relationship inevitably blurs the boundaries between personal and professional judgement. For the supervisor, this could lead to a failure to challenge poor practice on the part of the supervisee, leaving the clients at risk. Conversely, the counsellor could be vulnerable to his or her supervisor abusing their power and taking some personal revenge against them.

It may not always be the person who holds the greater power (therapist, supervisor or trainer) who initiates sexual activity. However, it is always the more powerful person's ethical responsibility to maintain the appropriate professional boundary, contain the development and keep the client, supervisee or student safe (BAC 1997). How this is done is important. Whether it comes from a client, supervisee or student, the reasons for rejecting any form of advance that may have sexual connotations should be made explicit, respecting the person's feelings and experience without shaming or pathologizing them (Bond 1993).

Whether sexual activity is permissible after the end of a professional relationship is a matter of ongoing debate. Those of psychoanalytic and many psychodynamic persuasions feel that sexual activity should never occur between former therapists and clients because of unresolvable transference issues. Practitioners from other theoretical approaches concerned about recognizing issues of adult autonomy may take a more liberal view. Vasquez (1991) points out that the option of a sexual relationship after therapy can contaminate the therapeutic work and the client's perception of therapy in the future. Francis (1999) also points out that although confidentiality continues after the end of the professional relationship, other professional and personal responsibilities, such as the duty of care or continuing concern, end. The general consensus of opinion is that there should always be a 'cooling off' period, preferably of several months or even years, in order for each person to review the relationship and allow time for reflection and consultation.

It may be argued that supervisory and training relationships are different from counselling in terms of activating transference. However, both kinds of relationship also involve an imbalance of power and influence, which may persist well beyond the formal end to the work. All therapeutic, supervisory and training relationships have expectations that the parties involved will behave with respect and integrity regarding issues such as confidentiality after the termination of work. Trainees and supervisees also expect to be able to ask for references. Such commitments may be seriously compromised by the development of a personal relationship to the detriment of the less powerful partner (Vasquez 1991). Again, it is for the therapist, supervisor or trainer to hold the major responsibility for the boundaries.

While reliable evidence is hard to find, it is likely that few practitioners start out with any conscious intent to introduce a sexual element to the professional relationship. Hunter and Struve (1998), quoting other writers, suggest that sexual boundary violations are best thought of as occurring through a process of decline from acceptable behaviour into erotic and unethical behaviour. POPAN list a number of common indicators that the therapeutic boundaries are being eroded and the work is in danger of becoming sexually inappropriate and unethical (see Appendix 3).

Therapists, supervisors and trainers need to recognize that a sexual attraction to a client, supervisee or trainee is not in itself unethical or simply a matter of 'erotic counter-transference'. The pull towards sexualizing a relationship may reflect something very important that needs to be therapeutically addressed. Practitioners need to be aware of their own sexuality, and their sexual and emotional needs and desires. They need to be able to recognize when these are activated and without acting them out (Spinelli 1994). They also need to be able to distinguish between a sexual attraction *towards* the client, which reflects their own process, and a sexual attraction *with* the client, which is the client's material (Woskett 1999: 195). The following quotation could usefully be extended to the supervisory and training relationships: 'It may therefore be taken as a rule that the more a patient or something in the analyst pushes for living out the sexual side of the relationship, the more probable it is that the sexuality is destructive' (Guggenbuhl-Craig 1971).

In order to avoid sliding down the 'slippery slope' into unethical involvement and behaviour, several writers (Guggenbuhl-Craig 1971; Lakin 1991; Spinelli 1994; Seto 1995; Webb 1997; Lamb 1999; Woskett 1999) suggest that practitioners need

- more training in awareness of sexuality in the interpersonal process, in ways of addressing and working with issues of sexuality in professional relationships and in how boundary dilemmas may be dealt with ethically;
- more self-awareness of their own sexuality, of their needs for intimacy and sexual satisfaction, and of how these may be met outside the working context; and
- more opportunities to discuss sexual feelings and experiences frankly and openly with a consultant or supervisor who can be trusted to help the practitioner explore and understand what is going on in a non-judgemental way.

Question 33

You get a student from a counselling course who, it becomes evident, is at present unsuitable to be practising as a counsellor and in your view should not be allowed to qualify because of unmanageable emotions or personal experience. The student is not inclined to report any of this to their tutor, who is not aware of the problem. How might this ethical dilemma be resolved?
Roger Casemore

It is not my place to make judgements about my client's suitability or otherwise to undertake a counselling course solely on the basis of my current experience of them in the therapeutic relationship. That is the responsibility first of all of the course staff and their selection criteria and processes and, second, of the client. That does not mean that I do not have concerns on the basis of my experience of his or her emotional condition and it is these concerns which give me an ethical dilemma arising from different ethical priorities.

Conflicts between ethical priorities are always problematic and in this case may be impossible to resolve satisfactorily. In this situation the ethical considerations which stand out most clearly to me are in respect of

- my relationship to my client and my client's right to confidentiality, autonomy and self-determination,
- the safety of my client in relation to the potential for that client, through their own vulnerability, to be damaged themselves by clients they might counsel,
- the likelihood of the client being open to complaint about their counselling,
- the safety of potential clients whom the client might offer counselling to,
- the safety of other students on the course with whom my client may practise,
- the responsibility of the tutors on the course for assessing their students,
- the possibility of my client bringing the counselling profession into disrepute,

- the autonomy and professional responsibility of the course tutors and
- the potential for my actions in this situation leaving me open to complaint.

As a person-centred therapist, for whom the six core conditions are both necessary and sufficient (Rogers 1957) my work is based on the principle of 'trusting in the wisdom of the client', staying with the client and whatever he or she wants to talk about and avoiding directing the client to talk about issues I want to discuss. However, two equally important principles contained in those core conditions are the need for the therapist to be internally congruent and the need for the therapist to be both genuine and appropriately transparent with his or her feelings in the relationship with the client.

I might begin by exploring with my client the nature of our relationship, perhaps sharing how we both feel the relationship is working. I suspect this issue, which is causing me so much concern, would be having some effect on the relationship and that it would be entirely appropriate for me to raise and discuss this, in a gentle, non-judgemental way. I must accept my client's wish not to inform his or her tutors about his or her current emotional state and personal experience. However, I would feel it appropriate to be sharing with my client my feelings of concern about the difficult position I find myself in and some sense of the dilemma with which I am faced. I would explore with him or her my concerns, particularly for his or her safety, arising from his or her current vulnerability. I would also express my concerns for the safety of his or her potential clients and for any students he or she may be working with in counselling practice on the course. It might also be appropriate for me to enable my client to explore his or her reasons for wanting to train in counselling, to help the client to consider how he or she might wish to pursue that goal and whether this is the most appropriate time to do that, bearing in mind his or her current emotional state.

As a counsellor, my foremost ethical concern is my relationship with my client and maintaining the confidentiality of that relationship and my client's right to self-determination and autonomy. I am not at liberty to take my concerns about this client to the course tutors, and to breach that confidence, just because I am worried and have concerns about the suitability of my client to be undertaking training as a counsellor. I could choose to worry about this on my own and try to rely on working with my client in the hope that a resolution will occur. This is a very lonely and dangerous position to put myself in, when I do not actually need to deal with it in complete isolation.

Together with raising the issue with my client, another step that I would take would be to discuss the matter with my supervisor, examining my concerns and how I am dealing with them with my client. I would seek to identify and talk through all the ethical issues and the range of options which are open to me and take some guidance from my supervisor as to what I should and should not do. It is important to remember that my supervisor can only offer me guidance and that at the end of the day I will have to make a decision for myself and take responsibility for that.

In reality, it is the staff of the training course my client is attending who have the principle responsibility, along with my client, for determining his or her suitability for training and qualification. While I may be knowledgeable about my client's emotional condition when my client is with me in the counselling relationship, it is likely that the course tutors will be experiencing my client in a very different context, where he or she may be a very different person. I have no evidence of that and there is no way that I can seek any.

So far I have only been considering this question on the basis that I am concerned about the unmanageable emotions my client has been reporting to me and it may be that I can live with taking no action. It may be different if I become aware that these emotions are seriously problematic for my client and those he or she comes into contact with, or if I become aware that he or she may have a serious mental health or psycho-pathological condition. In that case, the risk of causing serious harm to him- or herself or to others would present me with an opportunity for a different form of action.

In my contracting with clients I always inform them that they have the right to confidentiality within counselling, providing that what they tell me does not lead me to believe that they are contemplating causing serious harm to themselves or to others. I tell them that in those circumstances I will not necessarily maintain confidentiality. The BAC code (BAC 1997: B.3.4.) makes it clear that in exceptional circumstances such as these, a client's consent to a change in the agreement about confidentiality should be sought whenever possible, unless there are also good grounds for believing the client is no longer willing or able to take responsibility for their actions. The code goes on to state that the ethical considerations include achieving a balance between acting in the best interests of the client and the counsellor's responsibility to the wider community.

Therefore in the case of a client with serious pathological or emotional difficulties, about whom I have a strong belief that they are likely to do some real damage to others or to themselves by continuing to take part in a training course or by offering counselling to others, I do have some opportunity and perhaps even a requirement to take action. Again I would need to discuss this thoroughly with my supervisor before taking any action. I would also want to discuss it thoroughly with my client, hoping to get his or her agreement to allow me to discuss the matter with the course tutor.

I would probably want to talk with my client more directly about the nature of counselling and the code and his responsibility, under B.6.1.3, to monitor one's ability to function and not to counsel when one's functioning is impaired by personal or emotional difficulty or illness. I would also suggest very strongly that he or she should take this issue to his or her counselling supervisor and discuss it with them. If in my opinion the situation was serious enough to warrant it, I would also want to make it clear that if my client continued to counsel in his current condition, then I would see this as a breach of the code, which might lead me to take out a complaint against my client. At this point, if not earlier, I would also be needing to discuss with my client whether he or she should remain in a counselling relationship with me at all and whether he or she wished to terminate counselling or take a referral elsewhere.

Then, either with his or her agreement or without if I had not been able to secure that, I could make contact with the tutors and discuss the situation with them. I would probably do this on the basis of telling them about my feelings about this client and my concerns about his or her current psychological or emotional state. I would make it clear that this was a matter which only the tutors on the course and my client could make a decision about, unless it was so serious that I was actually contemplating making a complaint against my client. I would do my utmost not to give them any information that was not relevant. In fact I would probably not need to tell them anything about my client at all other than that I was very concerned about his or her psychological or emotional state and my view that he or she was not in the right place to be counselling. I would tell them that I had discussed the matter with my client and whether he or she had given me permission to approach them or not. I could only suggest that perhaps the course tutors might want to check that for themselves.

I would hate to be in this position but it is clear that there could be no easy resolution to this situation and it would be my responsibility to get my ethical priorities right and to achieve a balance between acting in the best interest of my client and my responsibilities to the wider community and to the profession. I suspect that in this case I would be 'damned if I do and damned if I don't'. My feeling is that in the end I would have to believe that I would have to do something and live with the consequences, rather than do nothing and hope that it would go away.

Question 34

What are the issues to consider when, having clarified the immediate boundaries between counsellor and client, trainer and trainee, or supervisor and supervisee, and a contract has started, it is then discovered that the pair have overlapping worlds?
Derek Hill

The question reflects the assumptive framework that has underpinned the development of personal, private, confidential psychotherapeutic services in the late 19th and 20th centuries (McLeod 1997). Formerly, healing, including that which we would think of today as the province of mental health services, was a public activity involving the participation of family and community. Vestiges of those processes can be found in the Mass and in the rituals of Armistice Day.

A moment's thought about the ethics and codes of conduct of the major professions will confirm that each holds central the privacy of the relationship with the client and the confidentiality of the content of that relationship. But solicitors play golf with their clients and in many settings doctors have a variety of other, non-professional relationships with their patients. In those professions privacy sometimes breaks down and confidentiality is breached, and there is legislation to deal with those situations. That is to say, bad and unprofessional practice is regarded as the consequence of the deliberate acts, or omissions, of a professional who can be brought to account. The general expectation is that a professional can be trusted to keep their professional working relationships, and the personal or commercial information involved, separate from their social relationships with their clients and other members of the community.

Today, the distinctive difference between the psychotherapeutic professions and other professions lies in the codes of ethics and practice of the former. Those codes vary considerably in the degree to which they are explicit about multiple relationships with clients, and about the nature and chronology of forbidden relationships. Almost all contain injunctions which imply that the practitioner inevitably acquires the means to control and exploit clients if other, non-professional, relationships exist with them. The origins of that perception lie in the descriptions of human functioning offered by psychoanalytic and psychodynamic theories, in which the unconscious shapes or modifies almost every aspect of behaviour (Sandler *et al.* 1997). It is reinforced by the many histories of exploitative relationships between highly acclaimed practitioners and their patients (Russell 1993). There is an ever-growing body of evidence that clients have suffered in this way as a result of an involvement in many different kinds of psychological therapy. Whether or not unconscious processes are used to explain to clients the hazards of multiple relationships with their therapists, there is now a widespread recognition that the dynamics of therapy create them (Austin *et al.* 1990). However transitory, the psychological therapies involve some degree of power imbalance between therapist and client, a measure of dependency, and certain differences between what the therapist knows and understands about the client's circumstances and needs, and vice-versa. That imbalance in power, and in the means of influence, can and does get transferred to any other relationship with the clients. Training and supervision relationships may involve similar processes and can create similar hazards. The codes of ethics and practice for therapy, practitioner training and counselling supervision establish checks and balances for the protection of both the individuals involved in those professional relationships.

... it is then discovered that the pair have overlapping worlds

This situation might result in previously established relationships taking on an exploitative quality in the way that has been described. But there is another hazard. 'Overlapping worlds' could signify that the individuals concerned

- already have information about each other,
- already have a direct or indirect relationship with each other or
- share a specific affiliation, with attendant privileges and/or obligations.

Any combination of these circumstances could exist. All have the effect of invalidating a working assumption on which many of us, particularly in urban settings, base our working lives – that new clients, trainees or supervisees will be strangers. If, in a particular instance, that assumption is false, four questions need to be asked:

- What does A know about B?
- What does B know about A?

- Do A and B know the extent of each other's knowledge?
- What is the power balance between A and B resulting from their overlapping worlds?

The questions highlight a characteristic of the processes involved in therapy, training and supervision. All three transactions depend on an internal transparency for their effectiveness. Typically, each depends on engagement in interactive processes based on a shared assumptive framework and the existence of mutually agreed and explicit purposes. 'At this moment we are strangers' implies a situation in which very little can be assumed about the other unless information is exchanged, or perceptions are explored. Specifically, the presumption today is that their personal worlds *do not* overlap.

If an overlap exists, and secrets about it are held by one or other of those involved, it is almost inevitable that the person concerned will also have secret purposes – hidden agendas. In that situation the meanings and significance of exchanges will be complex and sometimes obscure, and potentially at odds with the declared purposes of the working relationship. In particular, inappropriate influence over non-professional relationships could be sought and achieved.

Alternatively, if connections between client and practitioner already exist it is possible that the power relationships which result from those external connections could distort the professional relationship, intentionally or otherwise. Those distortions could disadvantage either client or practitioner.

The problem in both kinds of situation is that there are influences at work which do not get addressed within the professional relationship. This may be because they are unknown, overlooked or deliberately concealed. Whichever is the case, the ethical nature of the relationship is compromised. It must therefore be questioned whether it is ever ethical to presume that the relationship will be that of strangers at the beginning of the counselling, supervision or training of an individual.

The professional relationships involved in providing counselling, practitioner training and counselling supervision each place some form of restriction on the client's, trainee's or supervisee's freedom to negotiate the nature of differentials in power. They also limit access to personal information about the practitioner. Some therapeutic approaches require that the practitioner remains very largely an unknown quantity to the client (Langs 1998). The client-centred approach advocates the minimization of those differentials and a commitment to 'mutuality' (Sills 1997). Strict analytic practice allows no extra-therapeutic contact while client-centred practitioners are open to the proposition that, with careful negotiation, it is possible to accommodate both multiple professional roles and the combination of professional and social relationships. BAC has adopted codes (BAC 1995, 1996, 1997) which underpin patterns of good practice that assure the delivery of services which respond to the users' (professional) needs and avoid exploitative and harmful outcomes. The Association's codes expressly forbid counselling relationships that are concurrent with either training or supervisory relationships, but neither ban nor promote the generality of multiple relationships. This is a reflection of the very broad range of approaches to therapeutic work found among its members. The codes require a close scrutiny of the implications of multiple relationships, including those with former clients (BAC 1997: B.5.3). Be it a counselling, training or supervisory relationship, the practitioner has a responsibility to seek and make use of the perceptions of detached, senior practitioner colleagues, such as supervisors, when finding a response to actual or potential multiple relationships. As with the majority of ethical dilemmas faced, the identification of an appropriate response will depend on the most careful consideration of the detail of each and every different situation.

A final thought should be given to the social setting in which those professional activities are undertaken. An individual's network of relationships may involve hundreds of other people and, significantly, is likely to be lived out in many different geographical locations, including cyberspace, and at different times of the day, week or year. Today's society and its technologies encourage us to learn to live parallel lives – at work, at home, at the club or on the internet. Our skills in conducting the kinds of multiple relationships which were commonplace in our grandparents' days have diminished as the opportunity to live fragmented lives in many different arenas has grown. There is reason to believe that the separation of intimate, familial, social and workplace relationships is also growing because it frees those involved from the tensions, dilemmas and compromises that multiple relationships demand. It also reduces the cost of experiments in self-expression and low-commitment connections. It must be questioned whether an adherence to 'modern', individualistic cultural ideas and hermetically sealed psychotherapeutic relationships serve society well at a time when 'postmodern' thinking with its view of the 'relational self' gains ground (McLeod 1997). Perhaps the psychotherapeutic professions should be seeking solutions to the very real ethical dilemmas of multiple relationships by pushing to be as accommodating of them as possible rather than slamming the door against them in sometimes crude and arbitrary efforts to eliminate risk.

Question 35

What ethical considerations need to be taken into account when writing up client work for training, CPD, research and publication?
Carol Shillito-Clarke

Within the field of therapy, there is a long tradition of using client work to demonstrate competence and illustrate practice. Whether the therapist is a trainee, writing their first client study for their tutor, or a senior practitioner, writing for national publication, the fundamental ethical principle is the same: therapy is a confidential process that is primarily for the benefit of the client; the client has the right to make an informed decision about how they should be treated and to determine the boundaries of confidentiality around their material. Theoretically, therefore, the client can even refuse permission for the therapist to discuss their work in supervision or to keep notes. Hence the importance of the therapist being clear, in the initial contract or agreement, that there are necessary conditions without which they cannot work ethically (BAC 1997; BPS 1998; UKCP 1998).

The therapist has an ethical responsibility to develop, maintain and continue their professional practice (BAC 1997; BPS 1998; UKCP 1998). Recognizing the conflicting ethical requirements of respecting the client's confidentiality and maintaining safe practice, the BAC *Code of Ethics and Practice for Counsellors* states that 'the client's informed consent must be obtained wherever possible and their identity must be effectively disguised' (BAC 1997: B.3.5.4). The key concerns for every therapist who wishes to use their work with the client, for whatever reasons, are therefore

- their dual role in relation to the client,
- gaining the client's informed consent to the use of their work and
- disguising the client's identity effectively.

The therapist's dual role

Once the therapist decides to use a client's work for some purpose of their own, however valid, they take on a dual relationship with the client. Another set of goals is introduced which may not be compatible with those of the client. A conflict of interest and a potentially unethical situation can develop (Meara and Schmidt 1991). For instance, the client may wish to terminate work before there is sufficient information for the study or research project to be completed. Or the therapist may feel constrained to demonstrate adherence to a theoretical approach that is inappropriate to the client's therapeutic need. Because the therapist is in a position of power relative to the more vulnerable client and is using the therapeutic relationship to further a non-therapeutic purpose, the fidelity of the relationship may be compromised. When seeking the client's informed consent, the therapist needs to examine carefully their own motives and potential gains, and particularly how these might be incompatible with the client's needs. Such reflection is vital in order to avoid any unconscious bias or coercion.

Gaining the client's informed consent

Obtaining informed consent implies giving the client 'as much relevant information as possible . . . and to present that information in a supportive, noncoercive manner' (Meara and Schmidt 1991: 249). The information given, and the way in which it is given, must take into account the legal age of consent, the client's mental competence and their capacity for understanding the implications of any participation. The therapist must also take the responsibility for trying to identify possible sources of distress for the client and advising them accordingly. However, it is clearly not always possible to predict how the client may be affected, in either the short or the long term.

The point at which the client is asked for consent is important. Any information the client gains about the therapeutic process will affect that process positively or negatively. The major codes of ethics require that participants in any research project must give their informed consent in writing before the start of the project (BAC 1997; BPS 1998; UKCP 1998). It can be argued that a client study is a form of research and requires the same level of ethical rigour. On that basis, the client should be informed of any conditions affecting the therapy before it begins. They can then exercise their right to question any possible implications and choose what they bring to the work and what to withhold. Throughout the course of the work, they maintain the right to renegotiate the contract and withdraw their consent in the clear expectation that the therapy will continue without prejudice.

However, some therapeutic models suggest that the client should not automatically be fully informed about the process or the use to which their work may be put. It is claimed that, under certain circumstances, this could have an adverse effect on the therapy and therefore not be in the client's best interest. For example, it could affect the 'transference' or collude with the client's conditional need to be considered 'acceptable' or special. It is important that the therapist is aware of, and open to, the debate about when and how to inform the client. Above all, the therapist needs to guard against using theoretical arguments to justify a position of power or to avoid the discomfort of needing something from the client (Spinelli 1994; Gordon 1999).

In some cases, the potential value of the client's work as a study or piece of research only becomes evident as that work progresses. In such cases, the counsellor should be extremely cautious about seeking consent while therapy is in progress. A client who perceives the benefit of ongoing therapy and wishes it to continue can be particularly vulnerable, even to unintended pressure.

Asking the client's permission at the end of the work is also potentially difficult. Even if the client is given ample opportunity to discuss, reflect and make a clear choice to give or withhold consent, they may re-evaluate their therapeutic experience. This, in turn, may affect their faith in the fidelity of the counselling relationship, and may cause them to question whether or not they have been 'used', and for what reason ('why me?'; 'am I special?'; 'am I peculiar?'). At worst, the client may feel as if they have been exploited and psychologically harmed. The longer the gap between the completion of the work and the request for permission to use it as a case study, the more complex such issues may become.

Effectively disguising the client work

The extent to which confidentiality can be preserved through disguising key elements in the material is a serious question. The more the therapist needs to draw a picture of an individual client's history and circumstances in order to demonstrate how and why they worked as they did, the more likely it is that the client will be identifiable.

As Bond (1993) points out, a further question is, identifiable to whom? Even if the therapist knows who will read the work, it is difficult to be certain that the client is not identifiable. A constellation of details, which may not be significant to the writer, may be meaningful to the reader. The problem is compounded by other circumstances, such as a therapist with a few clients or a client who is also a member, or potential member, of the same organization. Additionally, elements of the client's material or story may unwittingly identify others involved with the client such as a child, partner or work colleague who may not have been party to the original contract.

One further question is whether the client should be allowed to read the completed study that, in some cases, may contain significant amounts of the counsellor's personal process material and reactions to the client. It could be argued that such material is confidential to the counsellor, and that disclosure to the client may cause them distress and could therefore do harm.

Given the above, using the client's work without their consent may be tempting, particularly if it seems unlikely that the client, or anyone who knows the client, will ever come across the material or recognize it in its disguised form. However, to do so would be exploitative and unethical, and could result in psychological or emotional damage to the client. There could also be serious implications for the client's future experience of counselling, the counsellor's reputation and professional standing, and the reputation of the profession as a whole.

Question 36

What are the ethical arguments for making therapy a required part of counsellors' personal development?
Derek Hill

This is an issue over which the psychotherapeutic world is divided. The personal and professional development opportunities provided within a training period leading to a professional qualification must equip an individual to undertake casework competently and ethically. Counsellors' personal material, their needs and their responses to situations arising during casework contribute to its content and process. That may help or hinder achievement of the client's objectives. If counsellors are to avoid unhelpful or unethical forms of involvement in casework they need a profound understanding of themselves and a well-developed ability to control how they make use of themselves in their work. It is disputed whether that degree of personal development can only be provided through personal therapy.

While the direct experience of therapy from the client's perspective is generally acknowledged to be a helpful component of professional development, disagreement exists about whether or not it is in fact an essential feature of a counsellor's training period.

If ethical arguments are to be established for making personal therapy a requirement of the training period it must be shown that without such therapy a counsellor places clients at a significantly increased risk of exposure to incompetent or unethical practice. The technical grounds for asserting the unique developmental benefits of personal therapy must therefore be examined. The detail of the developmental needs of a counsellor can be inferred from the relevant codes. While wordings differ, there is general agreement with the BAC *Code of Ethics and Practice for Counsellors*, which states that ethical practice requires that

- the counselling provided must 'facilitate the client's work in ways which respect the client's values, personal resources and capacity for choice within his or her cultural context' (BAC 1997: 3.1);
- 'Counsellors shall take all reasonable steps to monitor and develop their own competence and to work within the limits of that competence' (BAC 1997: A.6);
- 'Counsellors have a responsibility to consider and address their own prejudices and stereotyping attitudes and behaviour and particularly to consider ways in which these may be affecting the counselling relationship and influencing their responses' (BAC 1997: B.2.4);
- 'Counsellors are responsible for ensuring that their relationships with clients are not unduly influenced by their own emotional needs' (BAC 1997: B.6.1.5).

Self-knowledge and self-control have already been identified as necessary attributes of a therapist. The quoted clauses of the code indicate that counsellors must monitor the nature of their own involvement in the casework. Periodic reviews of the use being made of themselves would not protect the clients from their spontaneous and potentially distracting or destructive interventions. The monitoring required must be a continuous, background activity. Its outcomes must have a direct influence on the counsellor's behaviour within the casework so as to support and facilitate the client's purposeful work. Moment by moment, there is much about the client's and counsellor's joint work which is not known. As a result, there are almost always several ways in which to understand what is going on, and several options for action to be considered. This monitoring activity is commonly experienced as an internal dialogue, one which Casement (1985) described as taking place with an 'internal supervisor'.

The processes which contribute to this monitoring of casework are, among others,

- monitoring the counsellor's hidden self,
- monitoring the overt client–counsellor interaction,
- monitoring underlying themes and dynamics in the relationship,
- monitoring the client's thinking and emotions,
- hypothesizing on the basis of the perceived process and content of the counselling and on the states of the client and the counsellor,
- identifying options for the counsellor's action arising out of the hypotheses,
- selecting and implementing a preferred option for action and
- monitoring the impact of the action.

Monitoring is thus a complex and demanding activity. Learning to sustain that internal dialogue while remaining attentive to and engaged with the client is yet another skill that needs to be learned during the training period. Self-knowledge and the ability to choose one's actions are essential prerequisites. One psychodynamic approach to counsellor training sets personal therapy alongside a programme of experiential exercises developing theoretical understanding and technique, and counselling casework and its supervision, to respond to that threefold requirement (Jacobs 1991). Concerns that personal therapy based on a psychoanalytic model was not appropriate as a part of a family therapy and systemic training resulted in the integration of personal development and formal aspects of therapy training through the adoption of a sequence of experiential exercises (Hildebrand 1998). Relate's couple counsellor training has no requirement for personal therapy to be undertaken, although many trainees seek it of their own accord. The organization makes use of a combination of experiential exercises, 'awareness groups', as well as counselling casework and its supervision, to provide for trainees' personal and professional development (Relate 1999). Other psychotherapeutic trainings address the issue in different ways. An account by Johns (1996) illustrates the diversity of approaches that have been adopted in efforts to develop capacities to maintain self-awareness, monitor the counselling and intentionally shape it to serve the client's purposes.

The fact that so many dedicated and ethical trainers of counsellors and psychotherapists have elected to use different methods to promote personal and professional development invites the conclusion that there is no overriding evidence that only trainings which require personal therapy are effective and ethically sound. It is not even clear that they are the best trainings. Research has confirmed this conclusion. McLeod (1998) surveys the findings and indicates that, when compared with other strategies, trainings which require personal therapy offer no clear gain in terms of counsellor competence. Dryden *et al.* (1995) discuss self-development and reach the same conclusion while drawing attention to the importance of ensuring a concordance between the means adopted for trainees' self-development and the core theoretical model of the training programme.

If the technical argument for personal therapy as a requirement in order to achieve appropriate levels of self-awareness and process-monitoring is equivocal, it cannot be regarded as unethical not to require it. The ethical argument must rely on the proposition that an ethical training is one which offers the trainee the best opportunity to qualify as a competent practitioner. As has been indicated, those responsible for the counsellor-training, linked with the different core theoretical models, adopt a number of different means to provide that 'best opportunity'. And so the debate continues.

What of the need for the trainee to experience therapy from the client's viewpoint? It has already been acknowledged that experience of being in the client's role helps professional development. That broad endorsement of the proposition needs closer attention. Being a client offers the following potential benefits for the trainee counsellor:

- increased self-awareness,
- resolution of some personal issues,
- insights into enabling therapeutic strategies and interventions,
- awareness of the significance of the power differential between client and therapist,
- technique learned by example and
- awareness of the limitations of a therapeutic approach.

It can also result in

- trivialization of therapy (never engaged),
- counter-productive experiences of therapy and the therapeutic relationship,
- preoccupation with self,
- confusion about the boundaries and limits of therapy and
- alienation from the therapeutic process.

Other outcomes are possible, but those listed are sufficient to indicate that personal therapy may impede professional development as well as facilitating it. In particular, if the trainee participates in therapy on the basis of some course requirement rather than out of a sense of personal need, the negative outcomes may well outweigh the positive (McLeod 1998). It is arguable that course requirements which produce outcomes that disadvantage significant numbers of trainees are unethical and should be replaced by guidance which encourages trainees to take up personal therapy when they experience a need for it. The latter approach also has the virtue of underpinning the values reflected in clause B.2.2 of the BAC *Code of Ethics and Practice for Counsellors*: 'Counsellors are responsible for working in ways which respect and promote the client's ability to make decisions in the light of his/her own beliefs, values and context.'

In conclusion, the evidence available indicates that personal therapy can benefit trainee counsellors. It has value simply as a life experience. But that evidence does not support an ethical argument that personal therapy should be a required part of the training period for all counsellors. It follows that making personal therapy a requirement for those seeking accreditation or inclusion in a professional register cannot be justified on ethical grounds alone. When such a requirement is associated with an accreditation or a register designed to serve practitioners using any of a wide range of theoretical models it raises an ethical question. Is it ethical to stipulate that only one means of personal and professional development will be recognized when the trainings of the different approaches to counselling have developed a variety of effective ways by which individuals can achieve it?

An ethical case can be made for encouraging trainees to engage in a form of therapy concordant with their training, when they experience the need for it. In this regard couple counsellors and their trainers face the problem that a desirable component of the counsellors' personal and professional development may never be available to them because they have no partner or because, from an ethical viewpoint, priority must be given to avoiding infringement of their partners' civil liberties (Hildebrand 1998). In these situations a period of individual therapy is merely an option which should be considered.

Afterword

The ethical principles of responsibility, purposefulness, trustworthiness and confidentiality have been explored in as many contexts as is possible in a book of this size. The management of confidentiality has been a focus in counselling individual adults, couples and young people, in training, supervision and research, and within a number of settings. The complex issues of boundaries, overlapping worlds, dual and multiple relationships with clients, former clients, trainees and supervisees have been discussed. The emphasis on non-discriminatory practice has been a theme throughout many questions and explored more directly in several questions. The cornerstones of responsibility, competence and accountability and the requirements of proper conduct have also been recurring themes throughout. The purposeful nature of counselling has been highlighted, together with how counselling and therapy differ from other ways of helping people. The connection between standards of practice codified by various professional associations on the one hand and the universal moral principles on the other has been established.

The main difficulty when writing with reference to codes and guidelines is that professional associations revise their codes and guidelines periodically. We are aware that while writing this book BAC is looking at the possibility of a unified code with the superordinate principles of beneficence, fidelity, autonomy and competence.

There was insufficient space for an important question about whether it is ethical to work as a counsellor without membership of a professional association. Readers may also consider that other important questions were not included; we agree and rely on the hope that the varying ways of approaching ethical issues can be applied to any question of practice. The authors welcome your feedback.

In conclusion, the profession is likely to face many challenges in the twenty-first century. Understanding and maintaining ethical standards will always be at the heart of these challenges.

APPENDIX 1

Definitions

The following are the Association of Humanistic Psychology Practitioners' current (1999) definitions.

Counsellor

Someone trained to deal with immediate problems and crises which arise, such as bereavement, a broken relationship, a difficult marriage, a specific illness like cancer or AIDS, problems with children, alcohol/drug problems etc. Many counsellors also deal with long-term problems. Counselling can also be done on a couple, family or group basis. Some counsellors also use active techniques and give specific advice.

Counselling psychologist

A psychologist qualified in the theory and practice of counselling and psychotherapy, and also trained in the systematic application of psychological knowledge to their work with clients. S/he will normally have a first degree in psychology, as well as the British Psychological Society's Diploma in Counselling Psychology, or equivalent postgraduate qualifications. S/he will be accredited as a Chartered Psychologist on the Register of the BPS.

Psychotherapist

Someone with a specialised, professional and broad-based training and the ability to work in depth with clients, sometimes for two or three sessions a week and often over an extended period of time. Psychotherapists may use a wide range of approaches or may concentrate on one in particular. Short-term psychotherapists usually specialise in more intense work with clients but of limited duration.

The following are current definitions by the British Association for Counselling.

Counsellor

The British Association for Counselling defines a counsellor as someone who deliberately works to the definition of counselling in and within the ethical framework of BAC's *Codes of Ethics and Practice* (1997 AGM).

Counselling

People become engaged in counselling when a person occupying regularly or temporarily the role of counsellor offers or agrees explicitly to offer time, attention and respect to another person or persons temporarily in the role of client.

The task of counselling is to give the client an opportunity to explore, discover and clarify ways of living more resourcefully and toward greater well-being (BAC 1979).

APPENDIX 2

List of professional associations and how to contact them

Association of Humanistic Psychology Practitioners
BCM AHPP
London WC1N 3XX
Tel: 0345 660326 (answerphone)
Fax: 01348 840845

British Association for Counselling
1 Regent Place
Rugby CV21 2PJ
Information: 01788 578328
Office: 01788 550899
Fax: 01788 562189
Minicom: 01788 572838
Email: bac@bac.co.uk
Website: www.counselling.co.uk

British Association of Psychotherapists
37 Mapesbury Road
London NW2 4HJ
Tel: 0208 452 9823
Fax: 0208 452 5182
Email: mail@bap-psychotherapy.org
Website: www.bap-psychotherapy.org

British Association for Sexual and Relationship Therapy
PO Box 13686
London SW20 9ZH
Email: info@basrt.org.uk.
Website: www.basrt.org.uk

The British Psychological Society
St Andrews House
48 Princess Road East
Leicester LE1 7DR
Tel: 0116 254 9568
Fax: 0116 254 0787
Email: mail@bps.org.uk
Website: www.bps.org.uk

Confederation of Scottish Counselling Agencies
18 Viewfield Street
Stirling FK8 1UA
Tel: 01786 475140
Fax: 01786 446207
Email: cosca@compuserve.com
Website: www.cosca.org.uk

POPAN
Prevention of Professional Abuse Network
1 Wyvil Court
Wyvil Road
London SW8 2TG
Tel: 0207 622 6334
Fax: 0207 622 9788

UK Council for Psychotherapy
167–169 Great Portland Street
London W1N 5FB
Tel: 0207 436 3002
Fax: 0207 436 3013
Email: ukcp@psychotherapy.org.uk
Website: www.psychotherapy.org.uk

APPENDIX 3

Warning signs

An extract from the leaflet 'What to look for when you go into therapy' (1998) produced by the Prevention of Professional Abuse Network:

- Therapist talks much more than you do
- Uninvited home visits
- Close physical contact without consent
- Inappropriate questions about your sex life
- Unpredictable behaviour
- Threats and threatening gestures
- Insisting on their own way
- Making you doubt your sanity
- Therapist says too much about their personal life
- Sessions often go over time
- Usual fees are waived
- Therapist arranges to meet you socially

References

Accuracy About Abuse, website: www.accuracyaboutabuse.org

Asherst, P. (1993) Supervision of the beginning trainee, *British Journal of Psychotherapy*, 10(2).

Association of Humanistic Psychology Practitioners (1999a) *Code of Ethical Principles* and *Code of Practice*. London: Association of Humanistic Psychology Practitioners.

Association of Humanistic Psychology Practitioners (1999b) *Ethical Review Procedure*. London: Association of Humanistic Psychology Practitioners.

Austin, K., Moline, M. and Williams, G. (1990) *Confronting Malpractice: Legal and Ethical Dilemmas in Psychotherapy*. Newbury Park, CA: Sage.

Bollas, C. and Sundelson, D. (1995) *The New Informants: Betrayal of Confidentiality in Psychoanalysis and Psychotherapy*. London: Karnac Books.

Bond, T. (1993) *Standards and Ethics in Counselling in Action*. London: Sage.

Bond, T. (1997) Therapists' dilemmas as stimuli to new understanding and practice, in W. Dryden (ed.) *Therapists' Dilemmas* (2nd edition). London: Sage.

Bond, T. (1999) *Confidentiality: Counselling and the Law*. Rugby: British Association for Counselling.

Bor, R. and Watts, M. (1999) *The Trainee Handbook*. London: Sage.

Bowlby, J. (1988) *A Secure Base: Clinical Applications of Attachment Theory*. London: Routledge.

Bramley, W. (1996) *The Supervisory Couple in Broad Spectrum Psychotherapy*. London and New York: Free Association Books.

British Association for Counselling (1979, re-issued 1985) *Counselling: Definition of Terms in Use with Expansion and Rationale*. Rugby: British Association for Counselling.

British Association for Counselling (1984, 1990, 1992, 1993, 1996a, 1997) *Code of Ethics and Practice for Counsellors*. Rugby: British Association for Counselling.

British Association for Counselling (1988) *Code of Ethics and Practice for the Supervision of Counsellors*. Rugby: British Association for Counselling.

British Association for Counselling (1991) *Basic Principles of Counselling*. Rugby: British Association for Counselling.

British Association for Counselling (1994) *Individual Accreditation Scheme.* Rugby: British Association for Counselling.

British Association for Counselling (1995) *Code of Ethics and Practice for Supervisors of Counsellors.* Rugby: British Association for Counselling.

British Association for Counselling (1996b) *Code of Ethics and Practice for Trainers.* Rugby: British Association for Counselling.

British Association for Counselling (1998a) *How Much Supervision Should You Have?* Rugby: *British Association for Counselling.*

British Association for Counselling (1998b) Practice dilemmas, *Counselling,* 9(4): 279–80.

British Association for Counselling (1998c) *Counselling in Education – Guidelines on Counselling in Schools.* Rugby: British Association for Counselling.

British Association for Counselling (1999) Practice dilemmas, *Counselling,* 10(2): 107–9.

British Association for Counselling Information Guide 4 (1996, reprinted 1997) *Ethical Guidelines for Monitoring, Evaluation and Research in Counselling.* Rugby: British Association for Counselling.

British Association for Counselling Research Committee (1989) Evaluating the effectiveness of counselling: a discussion document from the BAC Research Committee, *Counselling,* 69.

British Association for Sexual and Relationship Therapy (1996, reviewed 1999) *Code of Ethics* and *Code of Practice.* London: British Association for Sexual and Relationship Therapy.

British Psychological Society (1998) *Code of Conduct, Ethical Principles and Guidelines.* Leicester: British Psychological Society.

British Psychological Society, Division of Counselling Psychology (1998) *Guidelines for the Professional Practice of Counselling Psychology.* Leicester: British Psychological Society.

Carroll, M. (1996a) *Counselling Supervision: Theory, Skills and Practice.* Guildford: Cassell.

Carroll, M. (1996b) *Workplace Counselling.* London: Sage.

Casement, P. (1985) *On Learning from the Patient.* London: Tavistock/Routledge.

Casement, P. (1990) *Further Learning from the Patient: The Analytic Space and Process.* London: Tavistock/Routledge.

Casemore, R. (1995) *Confidentiality and School Counselling – Occasional Paper Number 1.* Rugby: British Association for Counselling.

Casemore, R. (1999) Why can't we own our mistakes?, *Counselling,* 10(2): 94–5.

Confederation of Scottish Counselling Agencies (1996) *Statement of Ethics and Code of Practice.* Stirling: Confederation of Scottish Counselling Agencies.

Criminal Injuries Compensation Authority (1999) *A Guide to the Criminal Injuries Compensation Scheme 1996, Issue Number Two (4/99).* Glasgow: Criminal Injuries Compensation Authority.

Cunningham, R. (1997) When is a pervert not a pervert?, *British Journal of Psychotherapy,* 13(3).

Dalal, F. (1988) Jung a racist, *British Journal of Psychotherapy,* 4(3).

Davies, D. and Neal, C. (eds) (1996) *Pink Therapy: A Guide for Counsellors and*

Therapists Working with Lesbian, Gay and Bisexual Clients. Buckingham: Open University Press.

Dicks, H. (1967) *Marital Tensions*. London: Routledge and Kegan Paul.

Dryden, W., Horton, I. and Mearns, D. (1995) *Issues in Professional Counsellor Training*. London: Cassell.

Ellis, A. (1997) Dilemmas in giving warmth or love to clients, in W. Dryden (ed.) *Therapists' Dilemmas* (2nd edition). London: Sage.

Erikson, E. (1959) Identity and the life cycle, in *Psychological Issues*, Monograph 1.

Feltham, C. and Dryden, W. (1994) *Developing Counsellor Supervision*. London: Sage.

Fong, M. L. and Cox, B. G. (1997) Trust as an underlying dynamic in the counselling process: how clients test trust, in W. Dryden (ed.) *Key Issues for Counselling in Action*. London: Sage.

Forrest, L., Elman, N., Gizara, S. and Vacha-Haase, T. (1999) Trainee impairment: a review of identification, remediation, dismissal and legal issues, *The Counselling Psychologist*, 27(5): 627–86.

Francis, R. D. (1999) *Ethics for Psychologists: A Handbook*. Leicester: BPS Books (British Psychological Society).

Freud, S. (1914) On narcissism: an introduction, in *Selected Essays XIV*. London: Hogarth.

Friel, J. (1992) In the matter of the powers of Her Majesty's Inspector of Schools to inspect counselling in polytechnics, colleges of further education etc. Unpublished legal opinion obtained by the British Association for Counselling.

Friel, J. (1998) In the matter of the British Association for Counselling, the Association for Student Counselling and the Association of Colleges. Unpublished legal opinion obtained by the British Association for Counselling.

Gilligan, C. and Murphy, J. M. (1979) Development from adolescence to adulthood: the philosopher and the dilemma of fact, in D. Kuhn (ed.) *Intellectual Development beyond Childhood*. London: Jossey-Bass.

Gordon, P. (1999) *Face to Face: Therapy as Ethics*. London: Constable.

Guggenbuhl-Craig, A. (1971) *Power in the Helping Professions*. Woodstock, CT: Spring Publications.

Hawkins, P. and Shohet, R. (1989) *Supervision in the Helping Professions*. Buckingham: Open University Press.

Hedges, L. E., Hilton, V. W. and Caudill, O. B. (1997) *Therapists at Risk: Perils of the Intimacy of the Therapeutic Relationship*. Northvale, NJ: Jason Aronson.

Hildebrand, J. (1998) *Bridging the Gap: A Training Module in Personal and Professional Development*. London: Karnac Books.

Hill, D. (1999) Counselling issues from an organisational perspective: a confidential service, *Counselling Matters*, Vol. 1, No. 3: 13.

Hobson, R. (1985) *Forms of Feeling: The Heart of Psychotherapy*. London: Tavistock.

Holloway, E. (1995) *Clinical Supervision: A Systems Approach*. Thousand Oaks, CA: Sage.

Holloway, E. and Carroll, M. (1999) *Training Counselling Supervisors*. London: Sage.

Holmes, D. A., Taylor, M. and Saeed, A. (2000) Stalking and the therapeutic relationship: ongoing research, in *Forensic Update*, 60. Leicester: Division of Forensic Psychology, British Psychological Society.

Holmes, J. and Lindley, R. (1989) *The Values of Psychotherapy*. Oxford: Oxford University Press.

Home Office Guide (1996) *The Work of the Coroner (Gwaith Y Crwner)*. London: Home Office.

Hooper, D. (1996) Into the new millennium, in R. Woolfe and W. Dryden (eds) *Handbook of Counselling Psychology*. London: Sage.

Howard, A. (1998) Roads to professionalisation: dare we travel the integrity route?, *British Journal of Guidance and Counselling*, 26(2): 303–9.

Hunt, P. (1986) Supervision, *Marriage Guidance*, Spring: 15–22.

Hunter, M. and Struve, J. (1998) *The Ethical Use of Touch in Psychotherapy*. Thousand Oaks, CA: Sage.

Jacobs, M. (1991) *Insight and Experience: A Manual of Training in the Technique and Theory of Psychodynamic Counselling and Therapy*. Buckingham: Open University Press.

Jakobi, S. and Pratt, D. (1992) Therapy notes and the law, *The Psychologist*, May: 219–21.

Jenkins, P. (1997) *Counselling, Psychotherapy and the Law*. London: Sage.

Johns, H. (1996) *Personal Development in Counsellor Training*. London: Cassell.

Jones, C. and Syme, G. (1994) Maintaining standards of advertising, *Counselling*, 5(2): 90–1.

Kearney, A. (1996) *Counselling, Class and Politics*. Manchester: PCCS Books.

King, D. and Wheeler, S. (1999) The responsibilities of counsellor supervisors: a qualitative study, *British Journal of Guidance and Counselling*, 27(2): 215–29.

Kutchins, H. and Kirk, S. A. (1997) *Making Us Crazy: DSM – The Psychiatric Bible and the Creation of Mental Disorders*. London: Constable.

Lago, C. and Thompson, J. (1996) *Race, Culture and Counselling*. Buckingham: Open University Press.

Lago, C. and Thompson, J. (1997) Counselling and race, in S. Palmer and G. McMahon (eds) *Handbook of Counselling* (2nd edition). London: Routledge.

Lakin, M. (1991) *Coping with Ethical Dilemmas in Psychotherapy*. New York: Pergamon Press.

Lamb, D. H. (1999) Addressing impairment and its relationship to professional boundary issues, *The Counselling Psychologist*, 27(5): 702–11.

Langs, R. (1994) *Doing Supervision and Being Supervised*. London: Karnac Books.

Langs, R. (1998) *Ground Rules in Psychotherapy and Counselling*. London: Karnac Books.

Lemma, A. (1996) *Introduction to Psychopathology*. London: Sage.

Littlehailes, P. (1998) Counsellor in court, *Counselling*, 9(1): 16.

Macdonald, A. (1992) Training and outcome in supervised individual psychotherapy, *British Journal of Psychotherapy*, 8(3).

McGuire, A. (1997) *False Memory Syndrome: A Statement*. Rugby: British Association for Counselling.

McLeod, J. (1997) *Narrative and Psychotherapy*. London: Sage.

McLeod, J. (1998) *An Introduction to Counselling* (2nd edition). Buckingham: Open University Press.

McMahon, G. (1997) Counselling in private practice, in S. Palmer and G. McMahon (eds) *Handbook of Counselling* (2nd edition). London: Routledge.

McMahon, G. (1999) Reflective practice, *Counselling*, 10(2): 105–6 and (3): 193–4.

MacPherson of Cluny, Sir William (1999) *The Stephen Lawrence Inquiry*. www.official-documents.co.uk/document/cm42/4262/sh-01.htm.

Martindale, B., Morner, M., Rodriguez, M. *et al.* (eds) (1997) *Supervision and Its Vicissitudes*. London: Karnac Books.

Maslow, A. H. (1954) *Motivation and Personality*. New York: Harper.

Masson, G. (1992) *Against Therapy*. London: HarperCollins.

Meara, N. and Schmidt, L. D. (1991) The ethics of researching counselling/psychotherapy processes, in C. E. Watkins and L. J. Schneider, *Research in Counselling*. Hillsdale, NJ: Lawrence Erlbaum Associates.

O'Connell, B. (1998) *Solution-focused Therapy*. London: Sage.

Page, S. and Wosket, V. (1994) *Supervising the Counsellor: A Cyclical Model*. London: Routledge.

Palmer, S. (1999) Can counselling and psychotherapy be dangerous?, *Counselling*, 10(3): 179.

Palmer Barnes, F. (1998) *Complaints and Grievances in Psychotherapy: A Handbook of Ethical Practice*. London: Routledge.

Pearson, B. and Piazza, N. (1997) Classification of dual relationships in the helping professions, *Counsellor Education and Supervision*, 37(2): 89–99.

Prevention of Professional Abuse Network (1998) 'What to look for when you go into therapy' (leaflet). London: Prevention of Professional Abuse Network.

Relate (1999) *The Certificate in Marital and Couple Counselling (Theory and Practice). Course Synopsis*. Rugby: Relate.

Riegel, K. F. (1979) *Foundations of Dialectic Psychology*. London: Academic Press.

Rogers, C. R. (1957) The necessary and sufficient conditions of therapeutic personality change, *Journal of Consulting Psychology*, 21(2): 95–103.

Rogers, C. R. (1959) A theory of therapy, personality and interpersonal relationships, as developed in the client-centred framework, in S. Koch (ed.) *Psychology: A Study of a Science. Vol. 3, Formulations of the Person and the Social Context*. New York: McGraw-Hill.

Rowan, J. (1988) The psychology of furniture, in S. Palmer, S. Dainow and P. Milner (eds) *Counselling Reader*. London: Sage.

Russell, J. (1993) *Out of Bounds: Sexual Exploitation in Counselling and Therapy*. London: Sage.

Rutter, P. (1990) *Sex in the Forbidden Zone: When Men in Power Abuse Women's Trust*. Glasgow: Aquarian.

Rycroft, C. (1988) Comments on 'Jung a racist', *British Journal of Psychotherapy*, 4(3): 281.

Sanders, P. and Liptrot, D. (1993) *Basic Research Methods and Data Collection for Counsellors. An Incomplete Guide Series*. Manchester: PCCS.

Sandler, J., Holder, A., Dare, C., Dreher, A. U. (1997) *Freud's Models of the Mind: An Introduction*. London: Karnac Books.

Schon, D. A. (1973) *Beyond the Stable State: Public and Private Learning in a Changing Society*. London: Pelican.

Scoggins, M., Litton, R. and Palmer, S. (1997) Confidentiality and the law, *Counselling*, 8(4): 258–62.

Scottish Office (1998) *What to Do after a Death in Scotland*. Scotland: The Stationery Office.

Searles, H. F. (1955) The informational value of the supervisor's emotional experience, in H. F. Searles (ed.) *Collected Papers on Schizophrenia and Related Subjects*. London: Hogarth Press.

Seto, M. C. (1995) Sex with therapy clients: its prevalence, potential consequences, and implications for psychology, *Canadian Psychology*, 36(1): 70–86.

Shapiro, D. and Barkham, M. (1993) *Relate – Information Needs Research. Final Report to Department of Social Security*. Rugby: Relate.

Shillito-Clarke, C. (1996) Ethical issues in counselling psychology, in R. Woolfe and W. Dryden (eds) *Handbook of Counselling Psychology*. London: Sage.

Sills, C. (ed.) (1997) *Contracts in Counselling*. London: Sage.

Skynner, R. (ed. J. Schlapobersky) (1989) *Institutes and how to Survive Them*. London: Methuen.

Spinelli, E. (1994) *Demystifying Therapy*. London: Constable.

Sue, D. W. and Sue, D. (1990) *Counselling the Culturally Different* (2nd edition). New York: John Wiley and Sons.

Sutton, C. (1987) The evaluation of counselling: a goal-attainment approach, *Counselling*, 60: 14–20.

Syme, G. (1994) *Counselling in Independent Practice*. Buckingham: Open University Press.

Syme, G. (1999) New Zealand Association of Counsellors, *Counselling*, 10(4): 294–5.

Taylor, M. (1994) Gender and power in counselling and supervision, *The British Journal of Guidance and Counselling*, 22(3): 319–26.

United Kingdom Council for Psychotherapy (1998) *Ethical Requirements for Member Organisations*. London: United Kingdom Council for Psychotherapy.

United Nations Convention on the Rights of the Child (1999) Geneva, Switzerland: Office of the United Nations High Commissioner for Human Rights, United Nations Publications.

Vasquez, M. J. T. (1991) Sexual intimacies with clients after termination: should a prohibition be explicit?, *Ethics and Behaviour*, 1: 45–61.

Venier, K. (1998) Confidentiality and therapeutic practice, *British Journal of Psychotherapy*, 15(2): 229–38.

Walker, M. (1993) The aftermath of abuse: the effects of counselling on the client and the counsellor, *Counselling*, 4(1): 40–4.

Watchell, P. (1997a) Dilemmas in giving warmth or love to clients, in W. Dryden (ed.) *Therapists' Dilemmas* (2nd edition). London: Sage.

Watchell, P. (1997b) The non-improving patient, in W. Dryden (ed.) *Therapists' Dilemmas* (2nd edition). London: Sage.

Webb, S. B. (1997) Training for maintaining boundaries in counselling, *The British Journal of Guidance and Counselling*, 25(2): 175–88.

Wosket, V. (1999) *The Therapeutic Use of Self: Counselling Practice, Research and Supervision*. London: Routledge.

Index